JN300007

Hussein Chalayan
from fashion and back

Hussein Chalayan
from fashion and back

目次 | Contents

06　ごあいさつ | Foreword

09　ファッションにはじまり、そしてファッションへ戻る旅 | from fashion and back
18　A.《逸脱する流れ》| THE TANGENT FLOWS
20　B.《慣性》| INERTIA
22　C.《エアメール・ドレス》| AIRMAIL DRESS
24　D.《パノラマ》| PANORAMIC
26　E.《飛行機ドレス（エコーフォーム）》| AEROPLANE DRESS (ECHOFORM)
　　　《共感疲労》| COMPASSION FATIGUE
28　F.《アフター・ワーズ》| AFTER WORDS
30　G.《束の間の瞑想》| TEMPORAL MEDITATIONS
32　H.《アンビモルファス》| AMBIMORPHOUS
36　I.《不在の存在》| ABSENT PRESENCE
38　J.《リーディングス》| READINGS
40　K.《ビフォア・マイナス・ナウ》| BEFORE MINUS NOW
42　L.《明白なる運命》| MANIFEST DESTINY
44　M.《ジオトロピクス（屈地性研究）》| GEOTROPICS
46　N.《休息》| REPOSE
48　O.《場から旅路へ》| PLACE TO PASSAGE
50　P.《ゲノメトリクス（ゲノム測定）》| GENOMETRICS
52　Q.《ブラインドスケープ》| BLINDSCAPE
56　R.《111》| ONE HUNDRED AND ELEVEN
58　S.《麻酔》| ANAESTHETICS
60　T.《エアボーン》| AIRBORNE
64　U.《地からは離れられない》| EARTHBOUND
66　V.《無為な日々を過ごす甘美さ》| DOLCE FAR NIENTE
68　W.《ミラージュ》| MIRAGE

70　フセイン・チャラヤンとの対話［聞き手：長谷川祐子］
84　Hussein Chalayan Interview [Interviewed by Yuko Hasegawa]

94　対談後記［長谷川祐子］
96　Afterword [Yuko Hasegawa]

98　作家略歴 | Biography

Foreword

Hussein Chalayan is one of the most visionary designers working in fashion today. He is renowned for an innovative use of materials, meticulous pattern cutting and a progressive attitude to new technology. His pioneering work is motivated by ideas drawn from disciplines not readily associated with fashion, crossing between anthropology, history, science, philosophy and technology. Chalayan is guided by what happens in the world, and by what engages him personally, and these concepts inform ideas behind his collections. His acclaimed runway shows function as performance pieces which allow him to express important concepts.

Born in Nicosia, Cyprus in 1970, Chalayan was educated in Cyprus and later in London. In 1993, he graduated from Central St. Martins College of Art and Design in London where his highly inventive graduate collection, The Tangent Flows, caused a sensation. The collection featured decomposed silk dresses that had been covered in iron filings, buried in the ground for months and then exhumed. The collection later featured in the window of the London retailer Browns, and helped to launch Chalayan as a new designer with a reputation for innovation. He launched his own label in 1994 and, since then, has twice been named British Designer of the Year. Today Chalayan runs a studio in East London, he shows bi-annually in Paris and sells internationally. Over the last fifteen years, alongside his fashion collections, he has regularly extended his ideas into museum exhibitions and art installations. He has directed short films and designed costumes for opera and dance performances.

This book was published on the occasion of the Mr. Chalayan's first full-scale exhibition in Japan, which was held at Museum of Contemporary Art Tokyo from April 3rd to June 20th, 2010 and presents fashion collections, art and film projects created between 1995 and 2009. It explores Chalayan's creative approach, his inspirations and the ideas which subsequently influence his work such as genetics, technological progress, displacement, migrancy and cultural identity. Chalayan's work demonstrates his unique ability to combine beautiful and wearable clothes for today with an intriguing vision of the future.

Tokyo Metropolitan Foundation for History and Culture,
Museum of Contemporary Art Tokyo

ごあいさつ

フセイン・チャラヤンは、1994年のデビュー以来、ファッションとアートの2つの領域を横断的に活動するクリエイターの先駆者として多大な影響を与えてきました。一つ一つのコレクションに込められる、現代社会に対する文明史観的な批評性や魅力的な物語性、LEDやレーザー光線など最先端のテクノロジーを駆使した革新的なデザインは、英国ファッション・アワードの「デザイナー・オブ・ザ・イヤー」を2年連続で受賞するなど、国際的に高く評価されています。一方で、映像作品やインスタレーションを精力的に制作し、2001年イスタンブール・ビエンナーレや2005年ヴェネツィア・ビエンナーレなどの国際展に参加し、アートの分野におきましても高い評価を受けています。チャラヤンの表現は、従来のファッションという枠にはとどまらず、アート、建築、デザイン、哲学、人類学、科学といった複数の領域を横断して展開します。その根底にあるのは、私たちを取り巻く環境への批評的眼差しであり、とりわけ、テクノロジーや移動、文化的環境によって身体およびアイデンティティがどのように変容するのかを服を通して探究してきました。

1970年にキプロス島のニコシアで生まれたチャラヤンは、12歳のときにロンドンに移住します。その後、ロンドンのセントラル・セント・マーティンズ・カレッジ・オブ・アート・アンド・デザインで学び、1993年の卒業制作において、《逸脱する流れ》というコレクションを発表。数ヶ月間土の中に埋めたシルクのドレスを核とするその内容は、大きな反響を生み、ロンドンのセレクトショップ、ブラウンズのショーウィンドウを飾ることになり、それが翌年自身のブランドを立ち上げるきっかけになります。現在は、東ロンドンにスタジオを構え、年に2回パリにてコレクションを発表しています。

本書は、フセイン・チャラヤンの1994年から2009年までに発表された代表的なファッション・コレクションに、映像作品やインスタレーションを加え、彼のジャンルを超えた多面的な活動を日本ではじめて本格的に紹介した東京都現代美術館の展覧会を記念して出版されました。

公益財団法人東京都歴史文化財団　東京都現代美術館

凡例

・掲載作品は、「フセイン・チャラヤン―ファッションにはじまり、そしてファッションへ戻る旅」(会場:東京都現代美術館 会期:2010年4月3日-6月20日)の展示に即し、fig.A-fig.Wのテーマに分けて構成した。但し、本書にあるfig.Wは本展での実展示はなく、《ミラージュ》は東京都現代美術館の館内で上映された1998-2010年のファッション・ショーの記録映像の一部として紹介された。
・fig.Kは、本展展示では《ビフォア・マイナス・ナウ》と《アフター・ワーズ》との共同展示であったが、本書での紹介は《ビフォア・マイナス・ナウ》のみとした。
・図版は本展出品作品全ての図版ではない。
・解説原稿はデザイン・ミュージアムで作成された小冊子の原稿をベースにした。
・p.26《飛行機ドレス(エコーフォーム)》、p.27《共感疲労》、p.58《麻酔》については吉崎和彦が、p.64《地から離れられない》、p.66《無為な日々を過ごす甘美さ》、p.68《ミラージュ》については、Donna Lovedayが、それぞれ新規原稿を担当した。
また、p.30《束の間の瞑想》、p.53《ブラインドスケープ》については、吉崎和彦が加筆を行った。
・コレクションは開催シーズン、年号を、作品は制作年を明記した。
・映像作品には上映時間を明記した。
・作品の所蔵先はフセイン・チャラヤンの所蔵は省略し、それ以外を明記した。

Explanatory note

*The works covered in this book are from the exhibition Hussein Chalayan: From Fashion and Back (Museum of Contemporary Art Tokyo, April 3 – June 20, 2010) and sectionalized by its themes from Fig. A – Fig. W. Fig. W in this book featuring the newest collection MIRAGE is only addressed in the video archive of Hussein Chalayan's collections from 1998 to 2010 in the exhibition.
*Fig. K in the exhibition consists of the 2 collections: Before Minus Now and After Words however, this guide only features Before Minus Now.
*This book covers selective images of the works from the exhibition.
*Most of the texts are reprinted from the booklet published by the Design Museum in London.
*Newly written texts only for this guide are by Kazuhiko Yoshizaki for Aeroplane Dress (Echoform) on page 26, Compassion Fatigue on page 27 and An-aesthetics on page 58, and by Donna Loveday for Earthbound on page 64, Dolce Far Niente on page 66 and MIRAGE on page 68.
Kazuhiko Yoshizaki also added some notes for Temporal Meditations on page 30 and Blindscape on page 53.
*The season and the year are specified for each collection.
The time length is stated in each section of video installations.
*Image credits are noted in each section and the images stating no copyright belong to Hussein Chalayan.

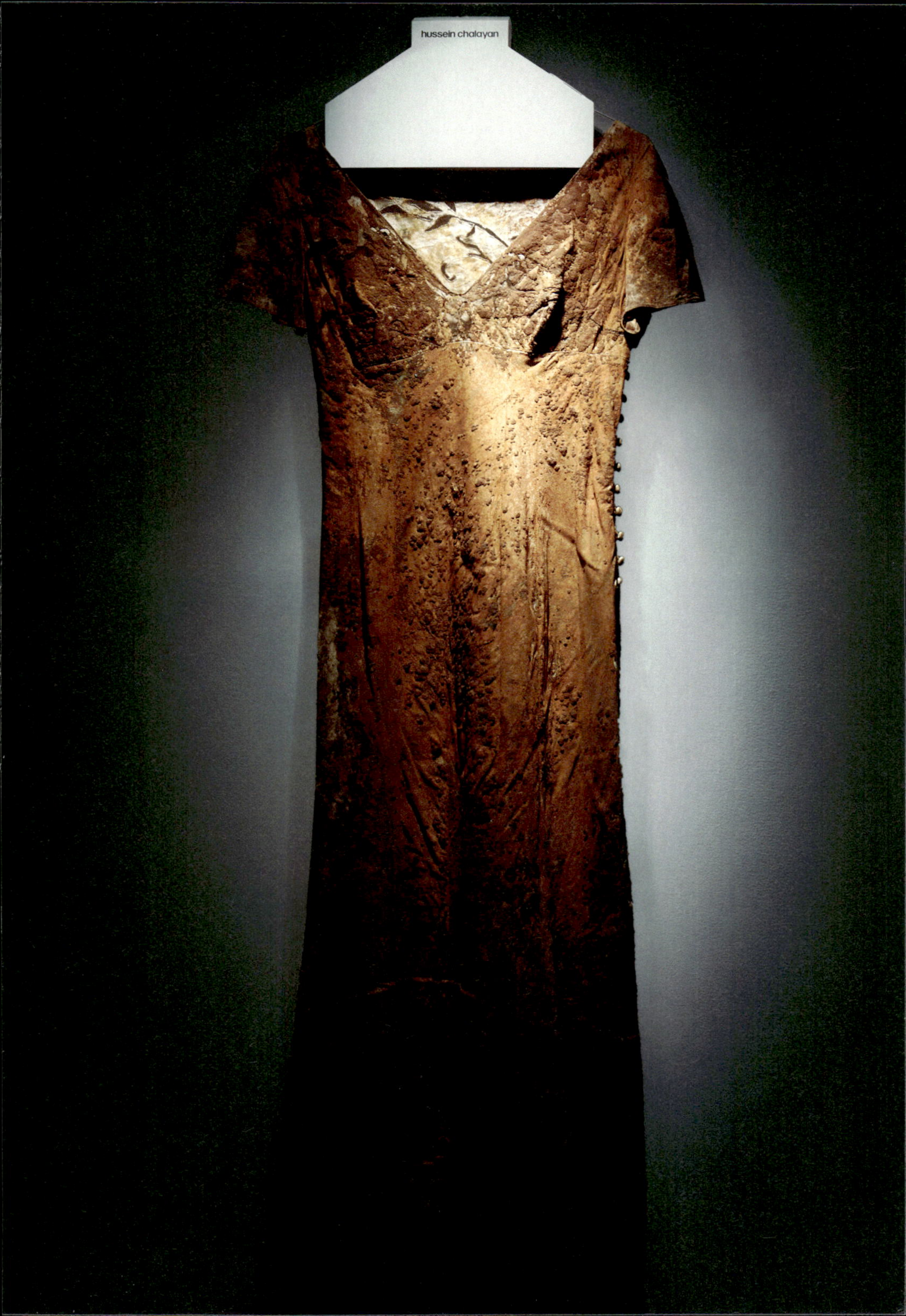
hussein chalayan

GEOTROPICS SS/1999

M

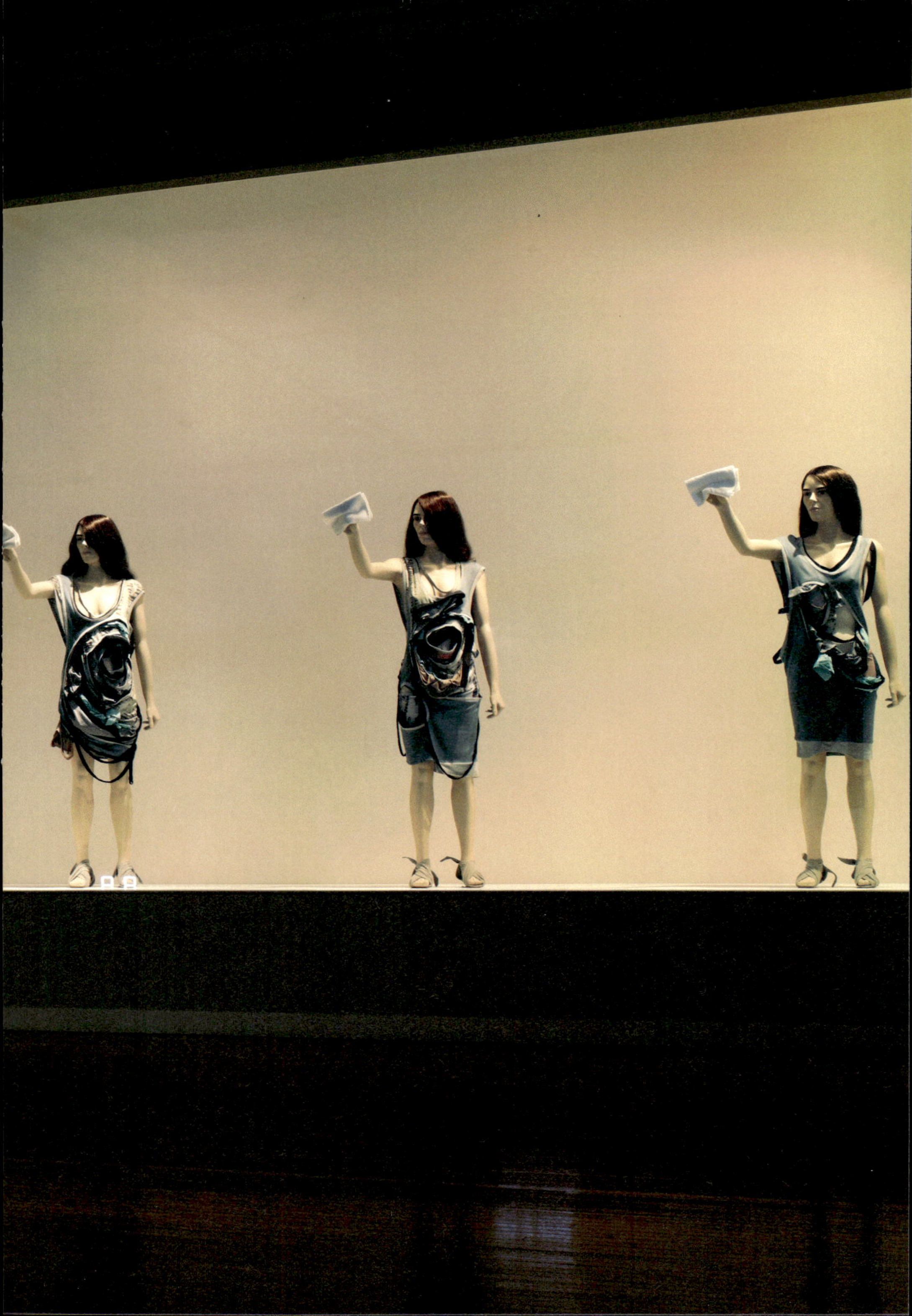

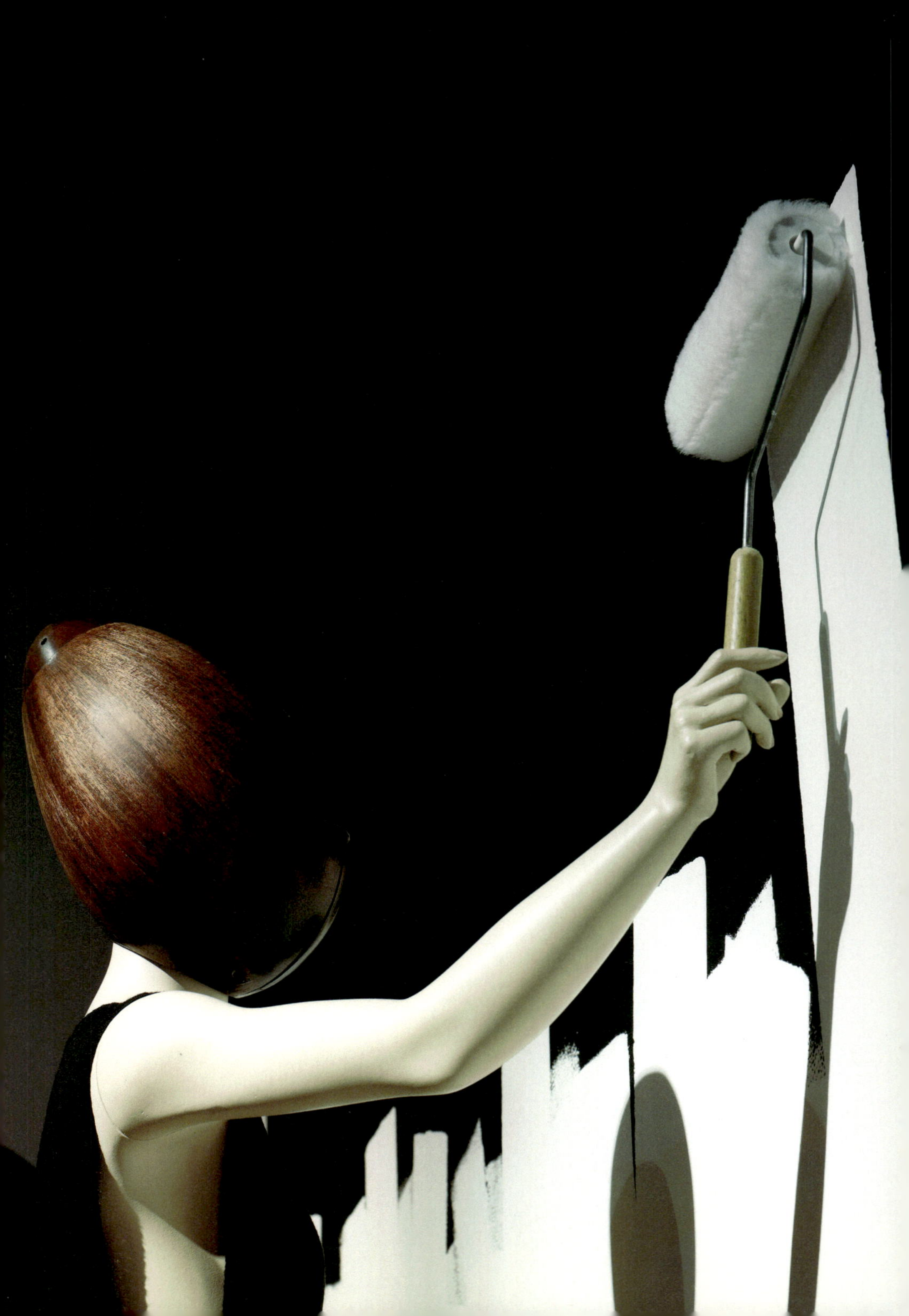

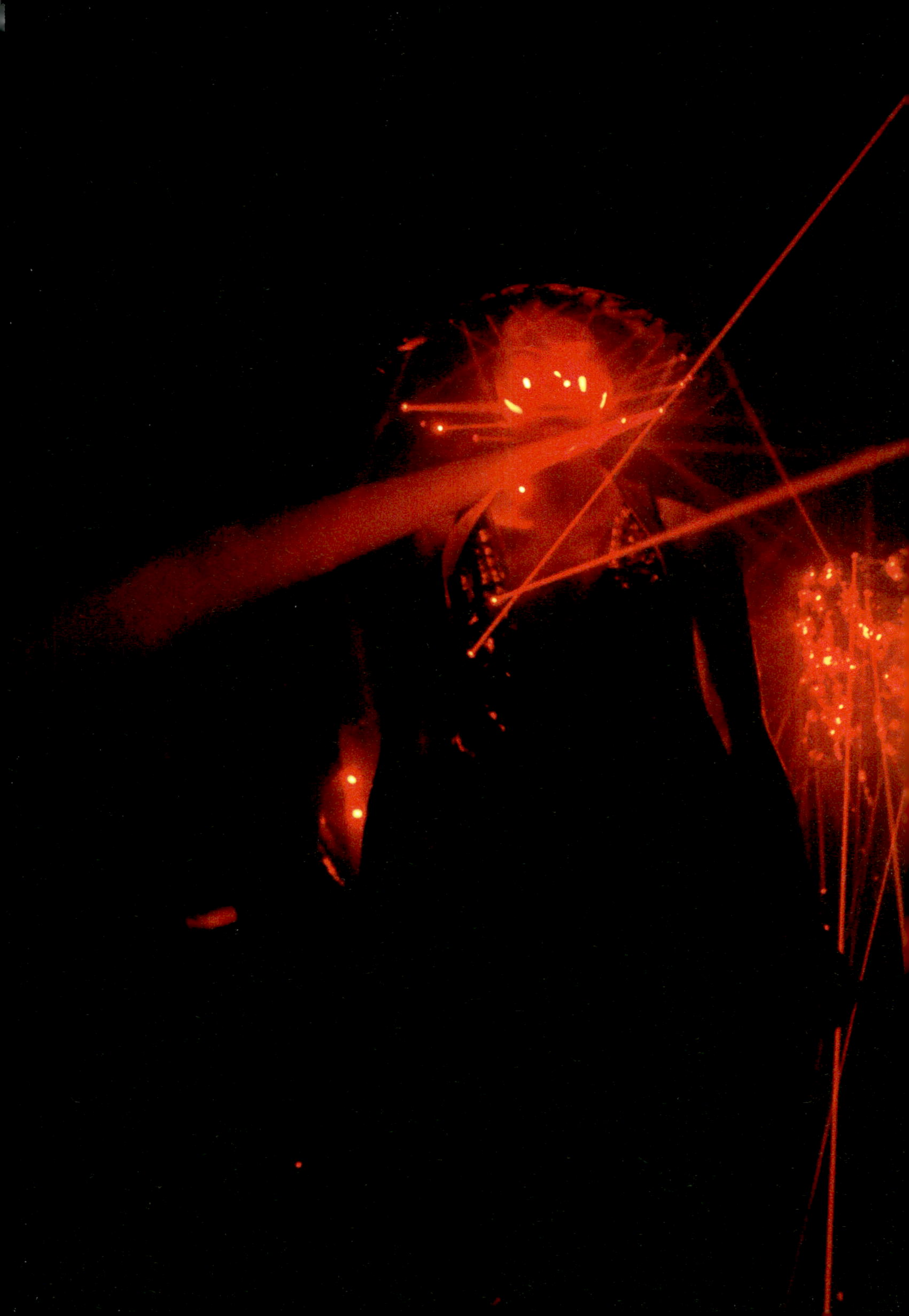

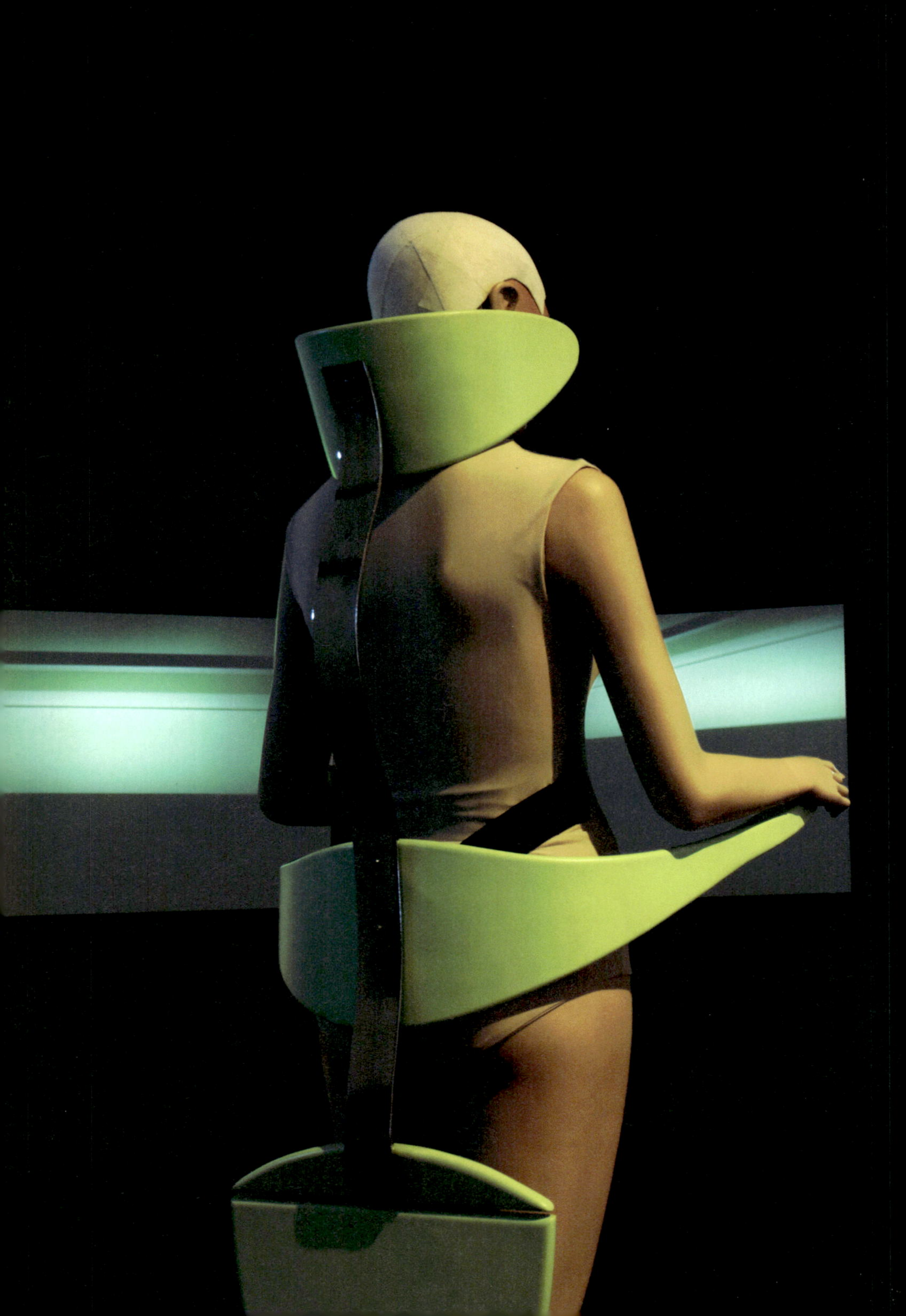

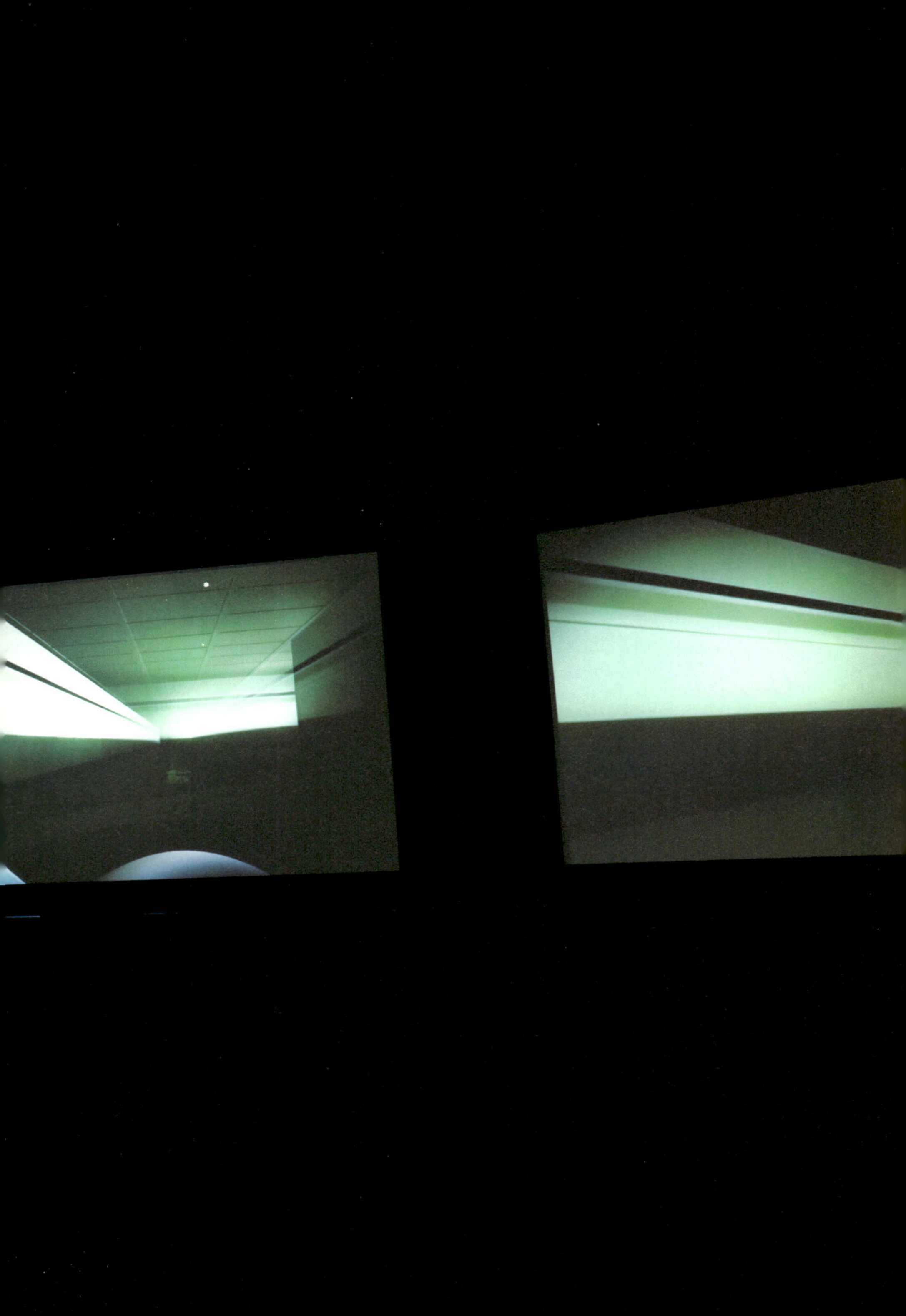

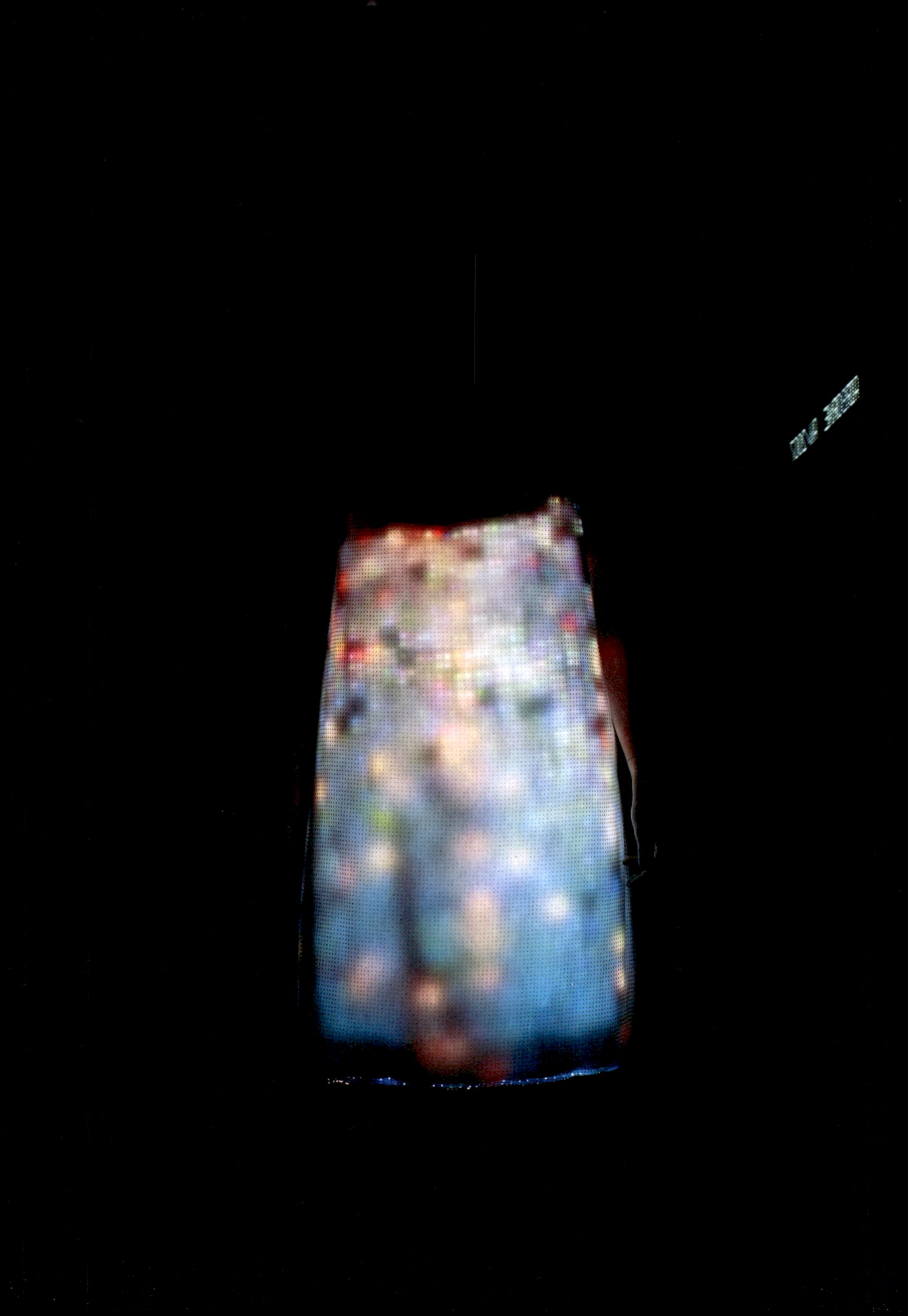

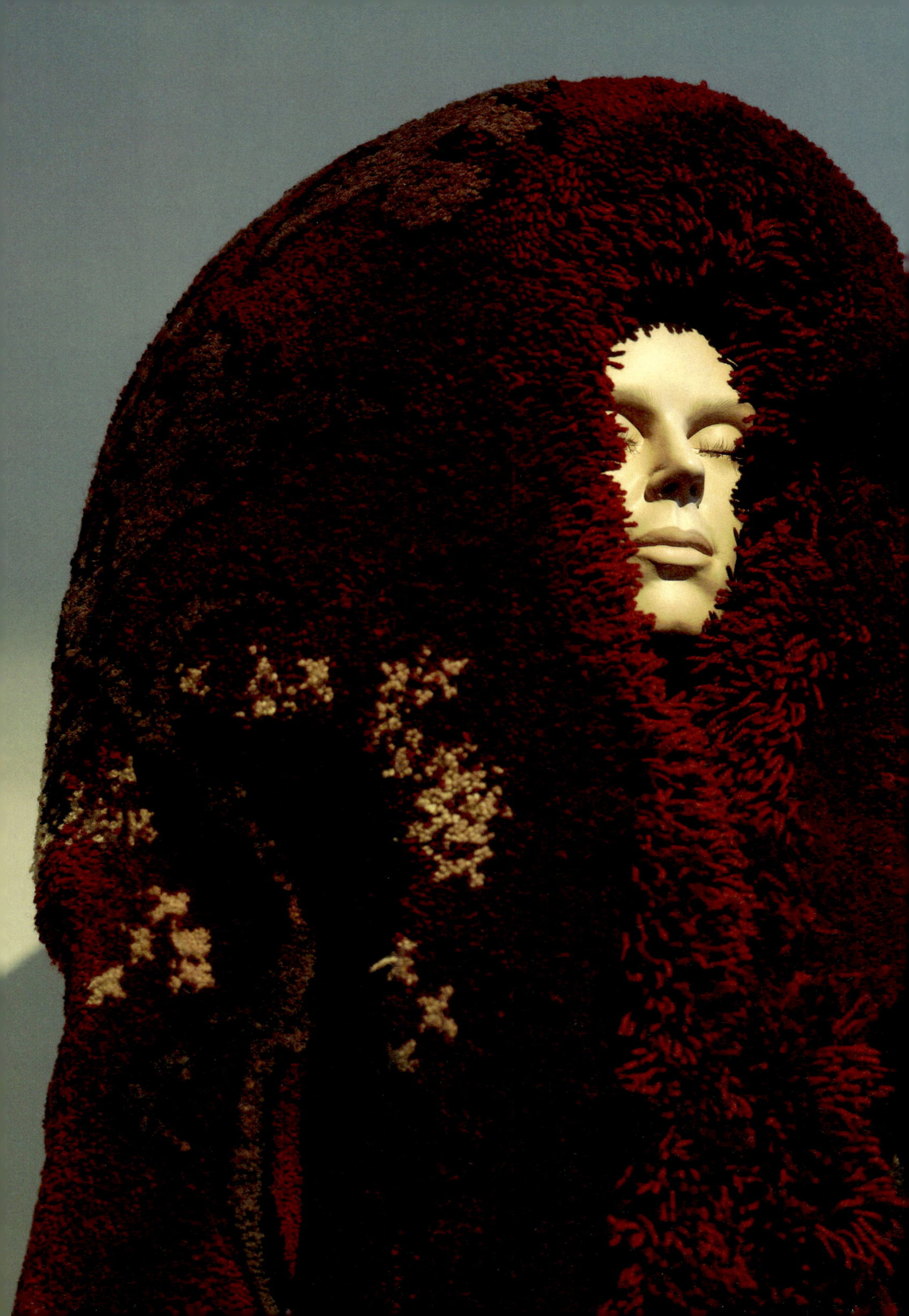

fig. **A**

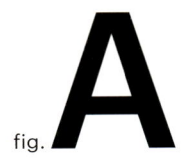

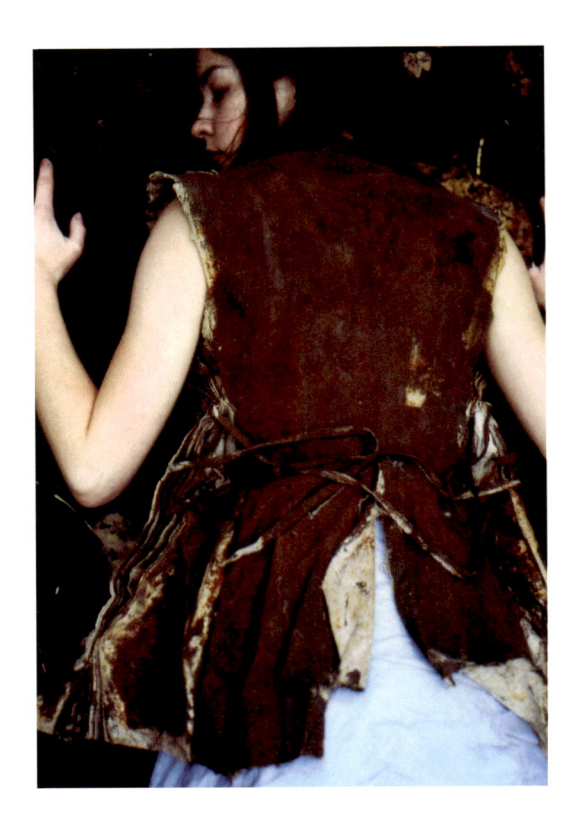

《逸脱する流れ》 | THE TANGENT FLOWS, 1993

ロンドンのセントラル・セント・マーティンズ・カレッジ・オブ・アート・アンド・デザインでファッションを学んだチャラヤンは、1993年の卒業制作において《逸脱する流れ》というコレクションを発表。数ヶ月間土の中に埋め、掘りおこしたシルクのドレスを核とするその内容は、大きな反響を生み、ロンドンの老舗ブティック、ブラウンズのショーウィンドウを飾ることになり、それが翌年自身のブランドを立ち上げるきっかけとなった。

In 1993, Chalayan graduated from Central St. Martins College of Art and Design in London where his highly inventive graduate collection, The Tangent Flows, caused a sensation. The collection featured decomposed silk dresses that had been covered in iron filings, buried in the ground for months and then exhumed. The collection later featured in the window of the London retailer Browns, and helped to launch Chalayan as a new designer with a reputation for innovation.

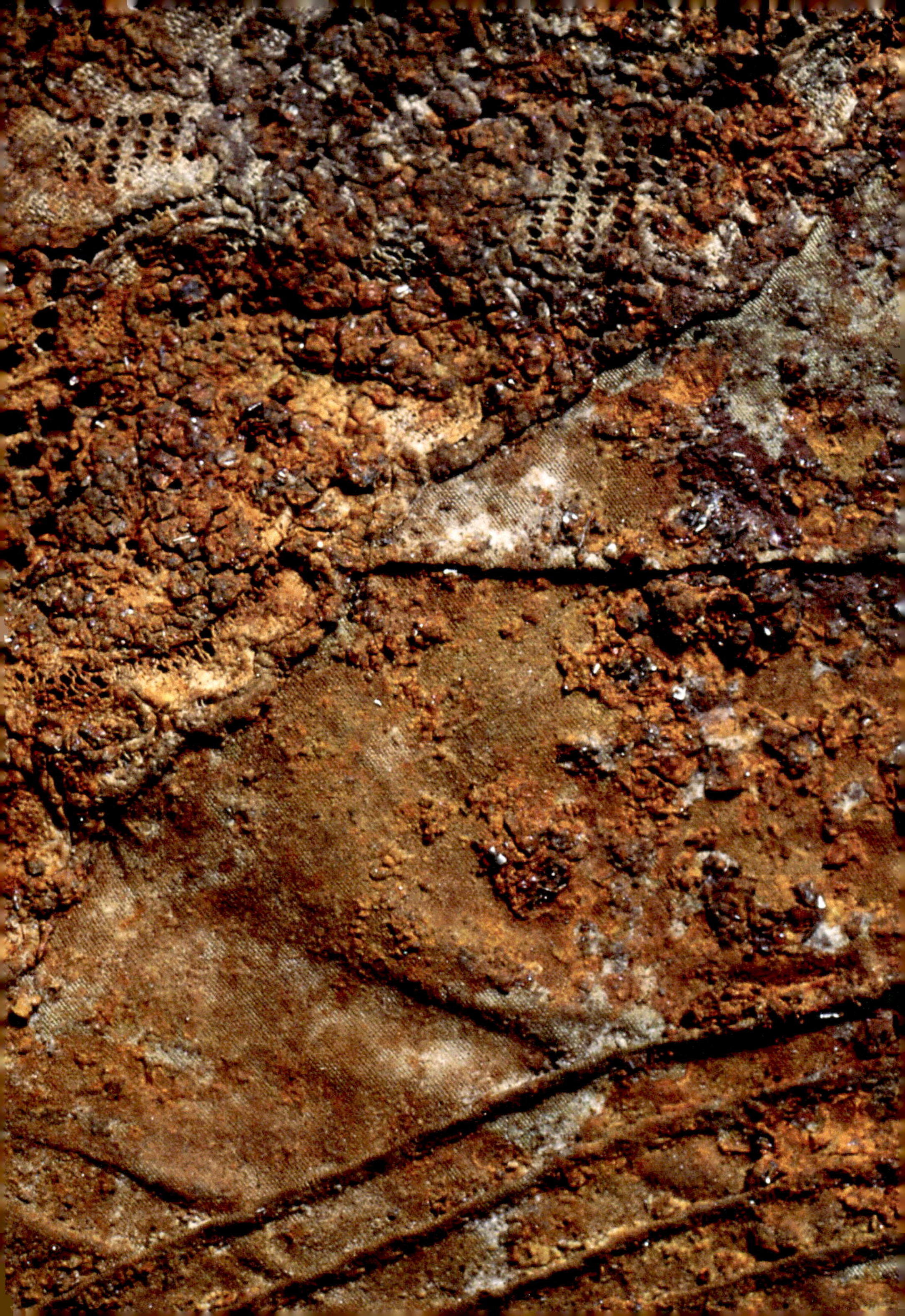

《慣性》| **INERTIA** (Spring/Summer 2009)

スピードは、生活のあらゆる領域において必要不可欠な要素となっている。デジタルコミュニケーション、旅行、商業はすべてスピードに左右され、ものの本質よりもむしろ、そのスピードによって善し悪しが判断されることも少なくない。ショーは、一つの流れをもって展開する。まず車の部品と身体内の空洞を表現する服に始まり、続いて、自然界を象徴するような有機的な形態をもつ服が登場する。ドレスの胸元には割れた車のフロントガラスが取り付けられている。最後のドレスは、まさに衝突の瞬間をあらわしている。スピードの真っ只中にあり、衝突の原因と結果は同じ時空間に包含される。これら3着のドレスには大破した車やナンバープレートのイメージがあしらわれている。

Speed has become the essence of every area of life. The pace of digital communication, travel and commerce are all charged by speed and achievement is often given merit by the speed through which it is born rather than the essence of what is being produced. The collection was envisaged as a sequence, beginning with the clothes carrying images of car components and body cavities. This was followed by a series of organic forms growing over the clothes to symbolise the natural world, which were then overtaken by aggressive images of broken windscreens. Finally, the body became the 'event' of a crash where garments caught in the midst of speed embodied the cause and effect of a crash in one moment, with garments bearing images of wrecked cars and number plates.

fig. B

fig. **C**

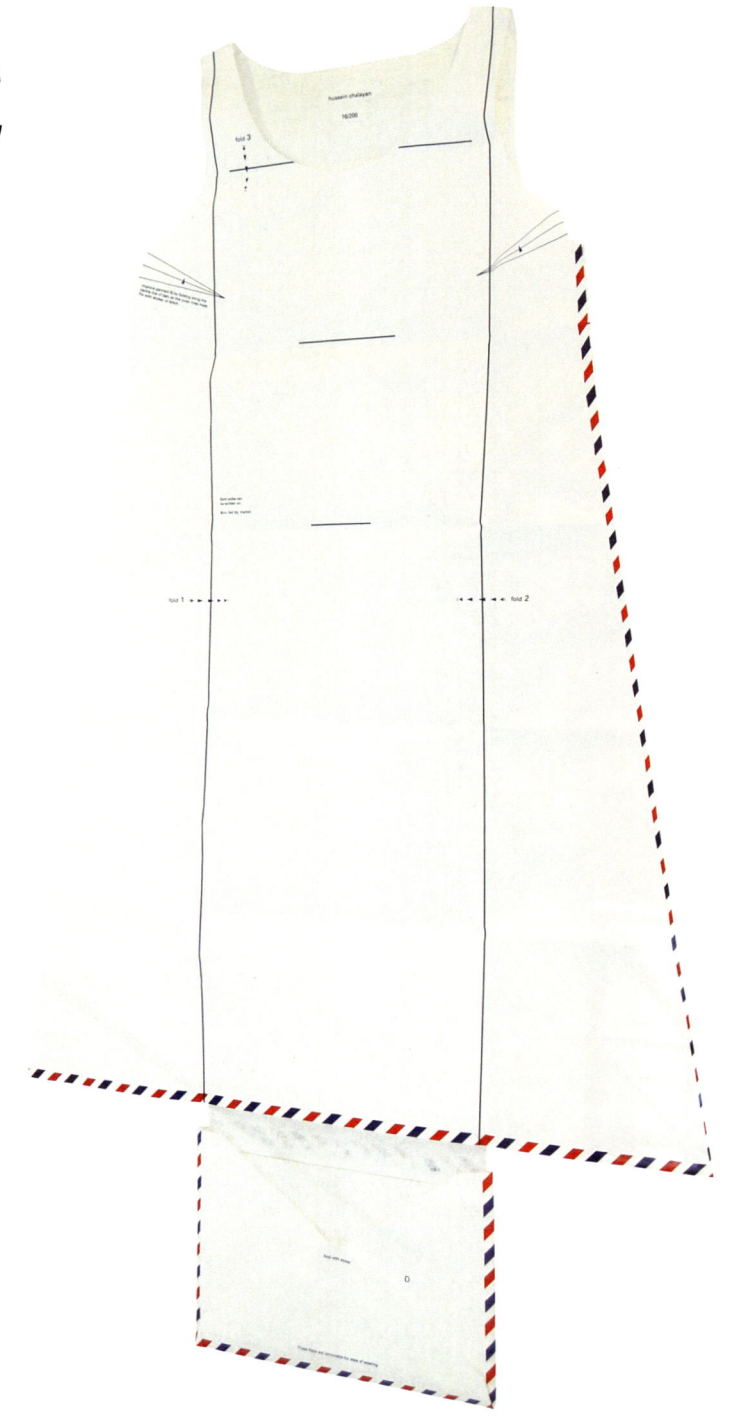

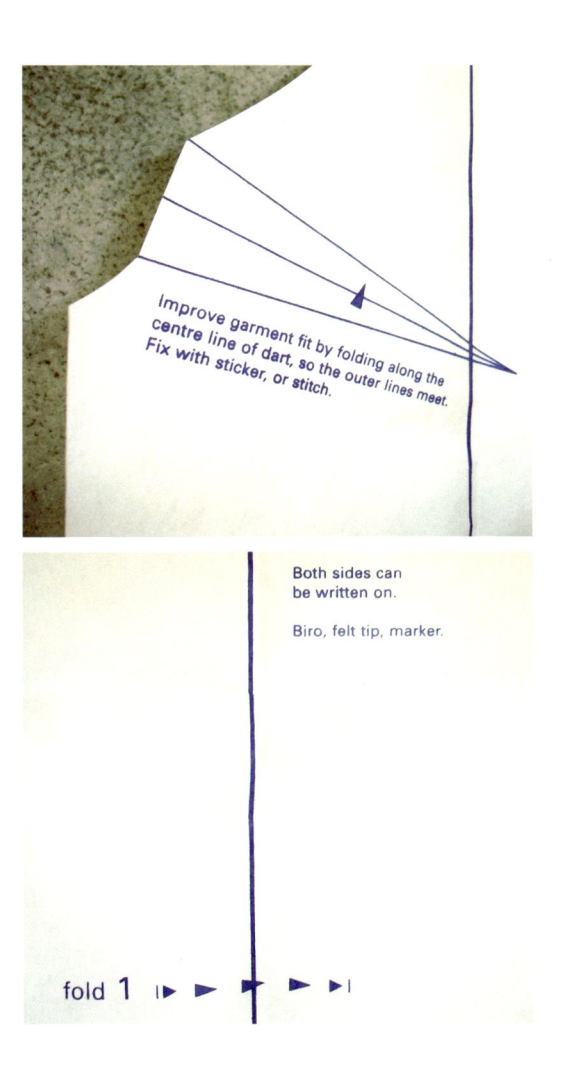

《エアメール・ドレス》| AIRMAIL DRESS (December 1999)

郵便で送ることのできるシリーズ第1弾が、このパッケージ化されたドレスである。このドレスには、折り方と着用方法を説明した指示書が付いており、一緒に郵送される。これを相手に送ることによって、ドレスはその人の不在をあらわすとともに、その存在のしるしにもなる。

The packaged dress was the first of a series that can be sent through the mail. The dress carries all the instructions for folding and fit. By sending it to another, it becomes a token of one's absence and presence.

fig. **D**

《パノラマ》| PANORAMIC (Autumn/Winter 1998)

本コレクションの出発点は「語りえぬものについては、沈黙せねばならない」*というオーストリアの哲学者ルートヴィヒ・ウィトゲンシュタインの言葉である。コレクションの核となるコンセプトは「カモフラージュ」。それは個人が完全に環境に溶け込んでいく過程で、あらゆる個性が失われていく様をあらわしている。これは言語や制度によって規定されているものを通じて、私たちがいかにアイデンティティを失っていくかについて言及している。本コレクションのショーでは、鏡が象徴的に用いられ、重要な位置を占めた。モデルたちは鏡の背後からキャットウォークに登場し、その姿は鏡に映り込み、歪められ、増殖し、そして鏡の裏へと消えていく。登場する服は定義しがたいものであった。民族衣装の要素を部分的にとり入れたものもあれば、あるいは制服を思わせるものもあり、そしてまた、昆虫を想起させる服もあった。このようにコレクション全体を通じてチャラヤンは、言葉では定義し得ないハイブリッドの創出を試みたのである。

*ウィトゲンシュタイン著(野矢茂樹訳)『論理哲学論考』岩波文庫 2003年 p.149

The starting point for this collection was provided by a statement by the Austrian philosopher Ludwig Wittgenstein, "Whereof we cannot speak, thereof we must be silent." At the centre of the presentation was the concept of camouflage in which the individual completely blends with the environment, apparently losing all individuality in the process. This was a comment on how we lose our identities through the parameters created by language and institutions. An important symbol in the presentation was the use of mirrors – models emerged from behind them onto the catwalk, reflected, distorted and multiplied, finally disappearing behind them. The clothes were deliberately difficult to define. Some were partially ethnic costume, some were a uniform, others an insect. Through the collection, Chalayan attempted to create hybrids which were indefinable through language.

Collection Groninger Museum, Groningen

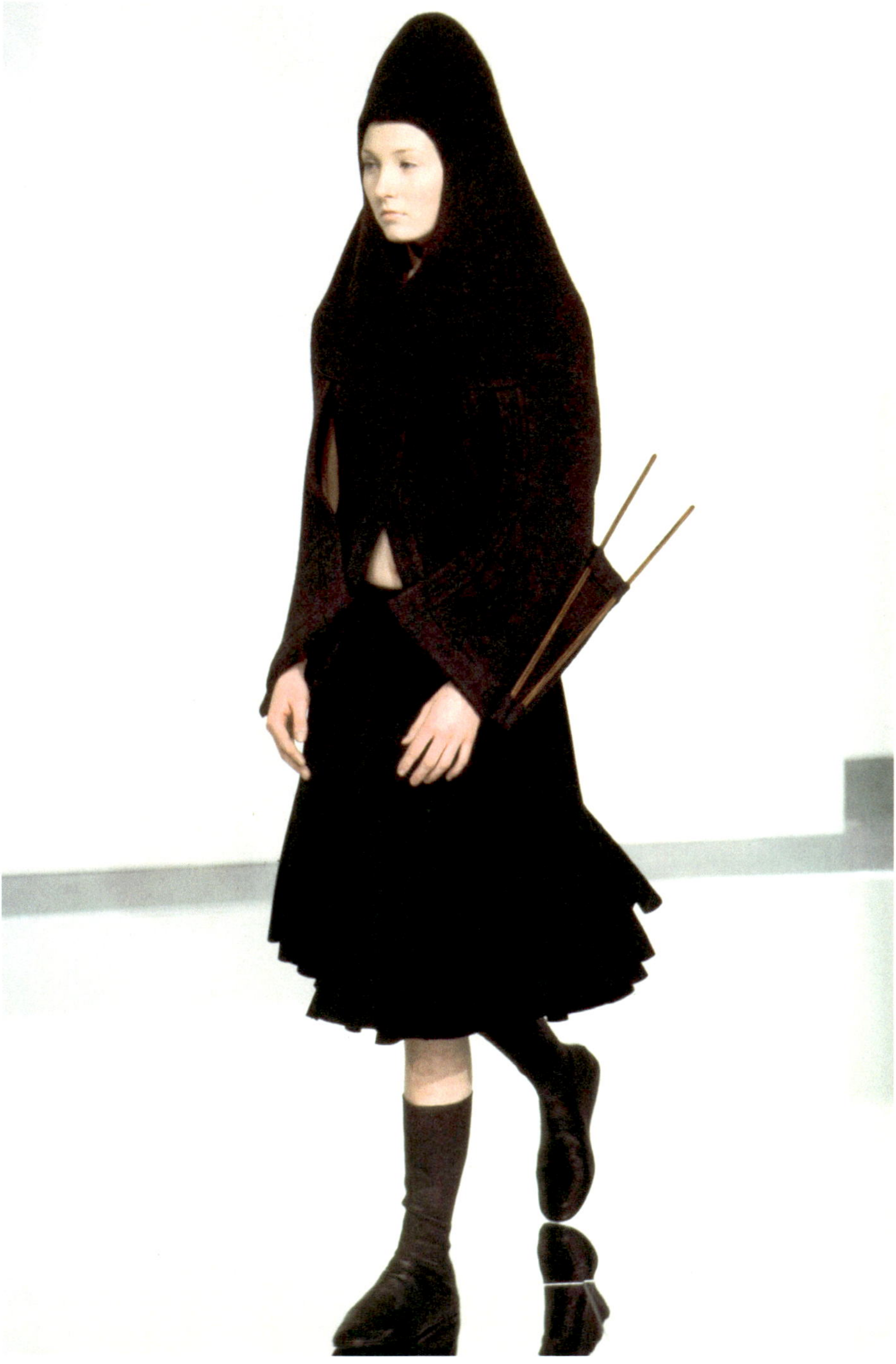

fig. **E**

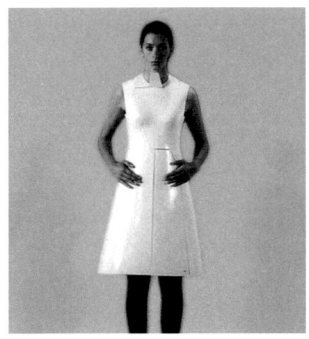

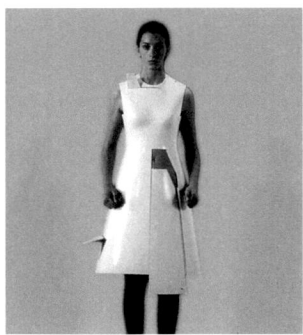

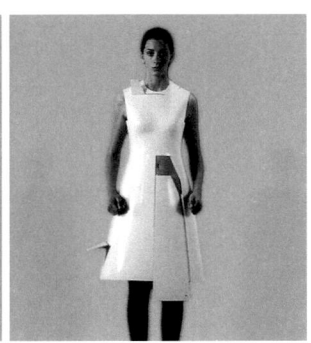

飛行機ドレス(エコーフォーム) | AEROPLANE DRESS (ECHOFORM), 1999

ガラス繊維と樹脂で作られた飛行機の機体を思わせるドレス。スカートに位置する翼のフラップのようなパーツが開くと、モデルが回転し始める。ゆっくりと、徐々に加速し、そして減速していくが、それは見る者に飛行機の離陸と着陸を想起させる。この飛行機というモチーフは、移動やスピードを象徴するものとしてチャラヤンの作品にしばしば登場するが、彼は単なるテクノロジーの礼賛に陥ることはない。そこには自身の経験に基づく"移住"や"亡命"といった負のイメージが常につきまとう。本作品では、イスラム教の礼拝の呼びかけを行うムアッジン(祈祷時報係)の声を背景に流すことにより、飛行機のイメージは直前に行われたアメリカ軍によるイラクへの爆撃と重なり合う。
［上映時間:2分18秒］

*本映像作品は、《エコーフォーム》(1999年秋冬コレクション)から「飛行機ドレス」をフィーチャーし、マーカス・トムリンソンがチャラヤンとのコラボレーションの下、制作したものである。

The dress is made of fiberglass and resin cast into a form that reminds us of a body of the aircraft. The skirt has parts that look like flaps on wings, and as they open, the model starts to turn around slowly. It reminds us of an aeroplane taking off and landing, as it turns around gradually more quickly and then more slowly. The aeroplane as a motif often appears in Chalayan's work as a symbol of movement and speed. Moreover, it is always shadowed by a negative connotation such as migration or exile. In this work, as the voice of a mu'azzin (the caller to prayer) calling Muslim prayers is played, the aeroplane's image is overlaid with the American bombing in Iraq which preceded the film.
[Duration: 00:02:18]

共感疲労 | COMPASSION FATIGUE, 2005

本作品は、人間と自然との関係を象徴的にあらわしている。どのように人間社会が自然を支配し利用してきたか、そして、人間の身体はその変化した環境にどのように適応してきたか。映像では、1人の女性をほかの3人の女性が取り囲み、呪文をかけることによって、その女性は大理石の彫像へと変身する。なお、4人の登場人物たちが着用している服は2006年春夏コレクション《ヘリオトロピクス》である。
［上映時間：4分27秒］

The work represents the relation between human beings and nature symbolically. How has human society dominated nature? How has the human body adapted to the changing environment? In the film, three women surround another woman, cast a spell on her and make her transform into a marble statue. The four characters wear clothes from his spring/summer 2006 collection entitled Heliotropics.
[Duration: 00:04:27]

《アフター・ワーズ》| AFTER WORDS (Autumn/Winter 2000)

fig. F

《アフター・ワーズ》は難民の苦境、そして戦時中に突然わが家を強制的に去らねばならない恐怖から着想を得たコレクションである。チャラヤンは、自身の家族を含むトルコ系キプロス人が、1974年国が南北に分裂する以前に、キプロスで民族浄化にさらされた過程を考察したことをきっかけに本作品を制作した。このコレクションは、そうした苦難に直面して家を離れる際に、所有物を隠そうとするのか、あるいはいっしょに持ち去りたいと切望するのか、その心理を探ったものである。リビングにはモダンな様式の椅子と円形のコーヒーテーブルが置かれ、そこでは服が椅子のカバーに、スーツケースが椅子に、そしてスカートがテーブルにそれぞれ姿を変えている。さらに部屋にある各オブジェはコートのポケットにぴったり収納され持ち去られる。モデルたちが部屋に入ってくるなり椅子のカバーをはずし、それを着始めると、家具は着用可能な服へと姿を変え、部屋はやがて空虚で生気のないものとなる。

After Words was inspired by the plight of the refugee and the horror of having to leave one's home suddenly in times of war. Chalayan took his inspiration from observing how Turkish Cypriots, including members of his own family, were subjected to ethnic cleansing in Cyprus prior to 1974 when the country was divided. The collection explored the idea of how people, when confronted by such an ordeal, want to hide their possessions or to carry them on departure. A living room was created with modernist style chairs and a circular coffee table. Within the room, clothes were disguised as chair covers, suitcases as chairs and a table as a skirt. Each object in the room fitted into a special pocket which was specifically designed to contain them. As models entered the room and began to clothe themselves, the furniture was transformed into wearable pieces with the room eventually becoming empty and lifeless.

Collection: Musée d'Art Moderne Grand-Duc Jean, Mudam Luxembourg

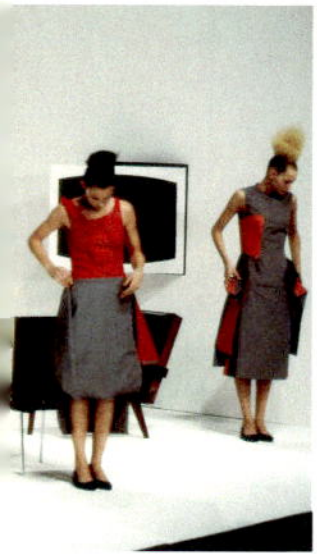

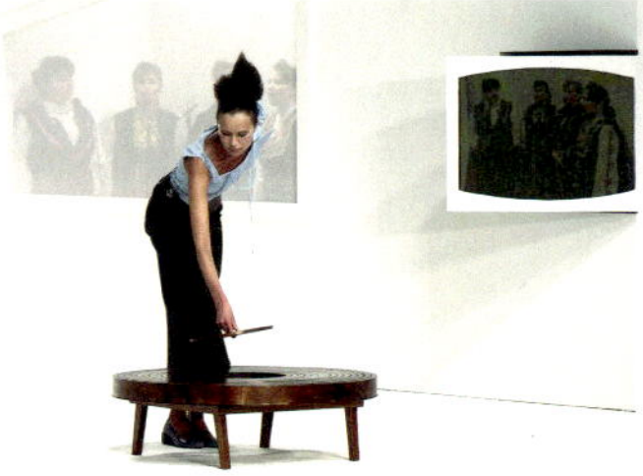

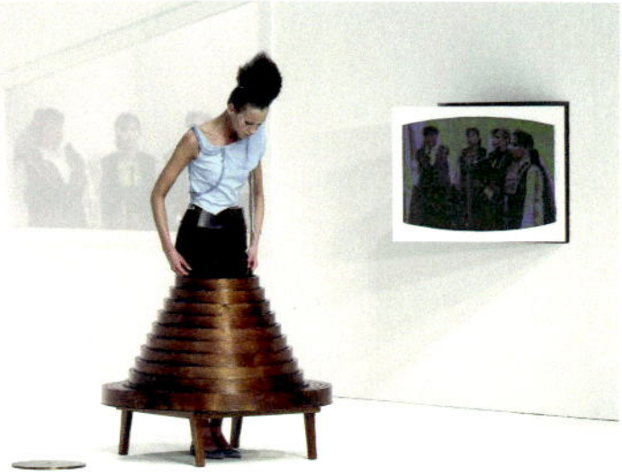

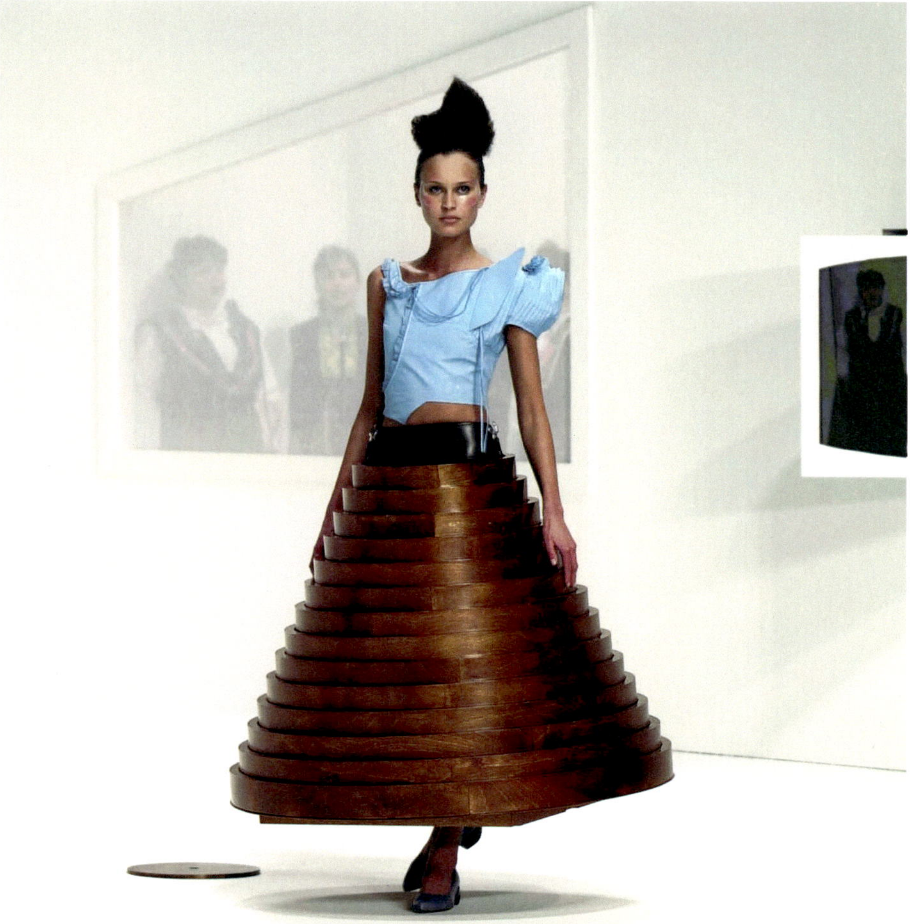

fig. G

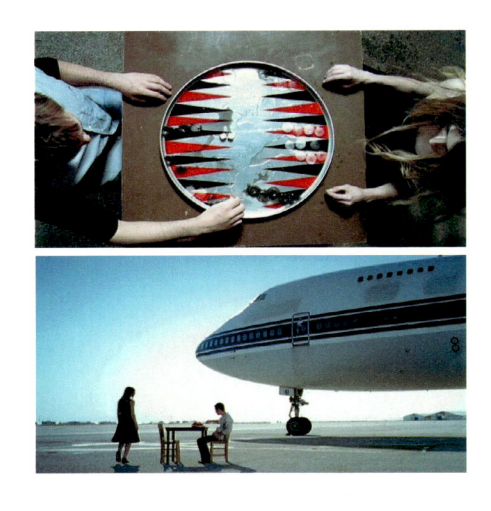

《束の間の瞑想》| TEMPORAL MEDITATIONS (Spring/Summer 2004)

歴史に関する言説は、時間を連続したものであり、常に前進するものとして示してきた。このことは、活字によって立証されてきたことである。本コレクションでチャラヤンが提示しているものは、彼の故郷であるキプロスを形作ってきた移住の歴史、その経路を辿ることで、過去と現在を結びつけることである。彼が、このような時空間をまたぐ民族移動を究明するための鍵として用いたのは、遺伝人類学。ここでの服は、過去と現在を繋ぐ考古学的なお守りとして、そして究極的にはそれ自体の考古学的探求において凍結された断片となるものとして捉えることができる。なお、本展覧会では、キプロスの歴史がプリントされた生地を用いたドレスを着ているブランコに乗ったマネキンと映像作品（上映時間：21分5秒）が、ドレスと同じパターンがプリントされた壁紙の貼られた空間の中に展示された。

Time has been defined as something sequential and progressive in discourses on history. This has been proved through letterpress printing. With this collection, Chalayan shows a potential connection between the past and present, by tracing the historical migratory routes which have formed his homeland Cyprus. He employs genetic anthropology as a key to determining the ethnic migration across space and time. The garments can be viewed as archaeological talismans which unite the past and the present. They become frozen fragments of their own archaeological quest in the end. In this exhibition, a mannequin in a swing, wearing a dress made of print with patterns showing history of Cyprus, was placed side by side with the film (Duration: 00:21:05). The wallpaper surrounding the installation was printed with the same pattern as the dress.

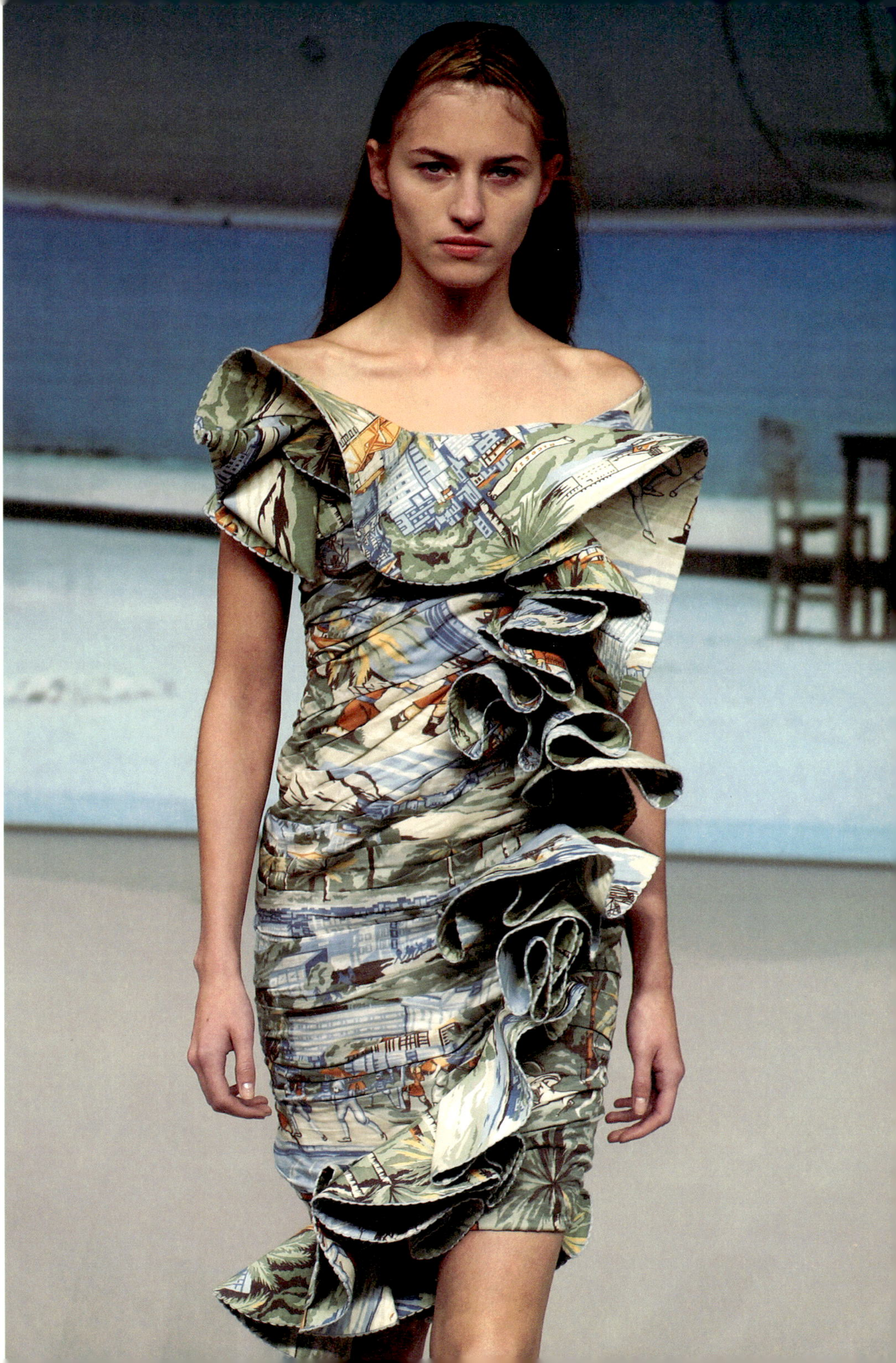

fig. H

《アンビモルファス》 | AMBIMORPHOUS (Autumn/Winter 2002)

《アンビモルファス》と名付けられたコレクションは、空間、時間、力、無力、有機的、機械的、民族的、モダンといった様々なコンセプトが立ち替わりあらわれる世界を巡る想像の旅と解釈できる。ショーにまず登場したのは、きらびやかな刺繍を施したトルコの民族衣装をまとったモデルだった。次々に登場するモデルの服からは"民族的な"要素が徐々に薄れ、長くて、モダンな"西洋的な"コートの黒にとって替わられる。その他の作品は"有機的"vs"機械的"のように対をなす組み合わせとなっている。繊維と革からできたドレスは、革が一種のハーネス(ロッククライミングで、クライマーがロープを体に結びつけるために装着する安全ベルトの一種)の役割を果たし、着ている者の動きを制御する。ショーのフィナーレは黒いドレスから始まり、それが冒頭に登場したような民族衣装へと変化していった。チャラヤンは映像作家のマーカス・トムリンソンとのコラボレーションで、この"変身"の過程をおさめた一連の写真作品を制作した。

The Ambimorphous collection can be interpreted as an imaginary trip through a universe in which a range of concepts such as space, time, power, powerlessness, organic, mechanical, ethnic and modernist all play a part. The show began with a model in a richly embroidered traditional Turkish costume. Other models followed wearing clothes whose 'ethnic' details were gradually usurped by the black colour of a long, modernist 'Western' coat. Other creations were combinations, such as 'organic' versus 'mechanical'. One dress was made of fabric and leather, in which the wearer's movements were restricted by the leather elements forming a kind of harness. The show's finale began with a black dress that changed into the ethnic costume which had started the show. Chalayan collaborated with video artist Marcus Tomlinson to create a series of photographs documenting the 'morph' process.

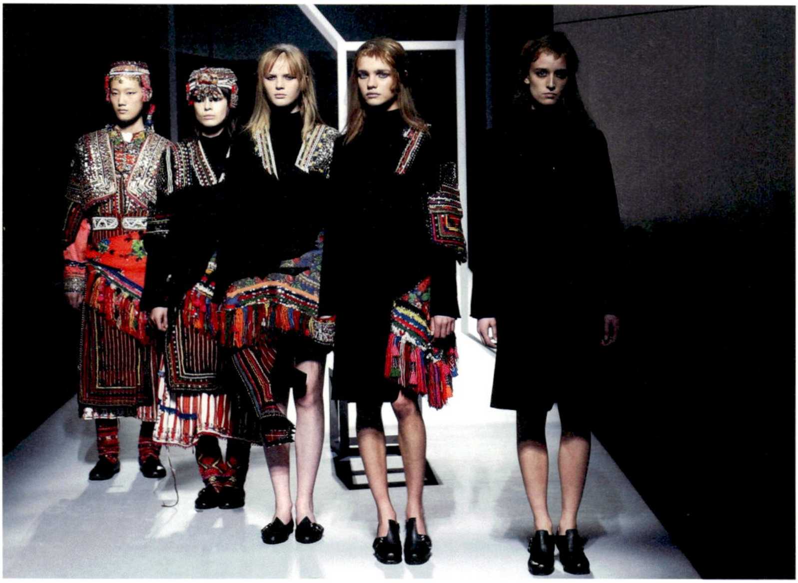

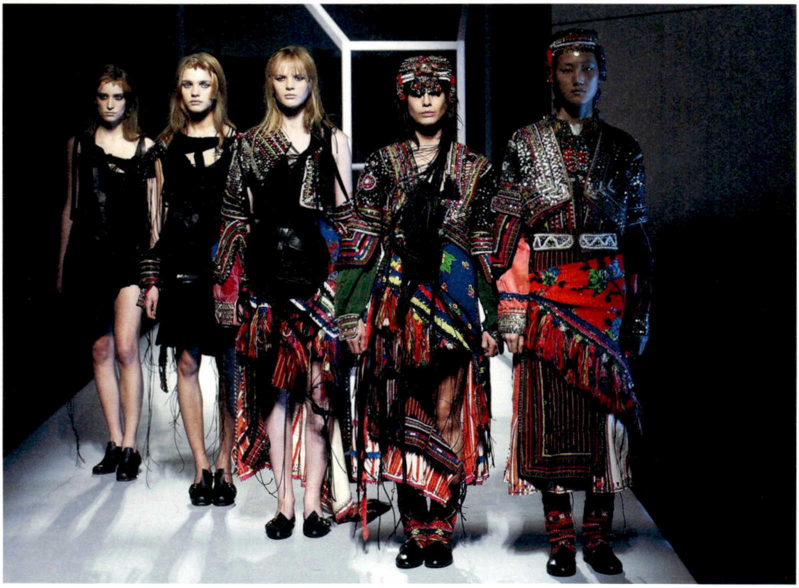

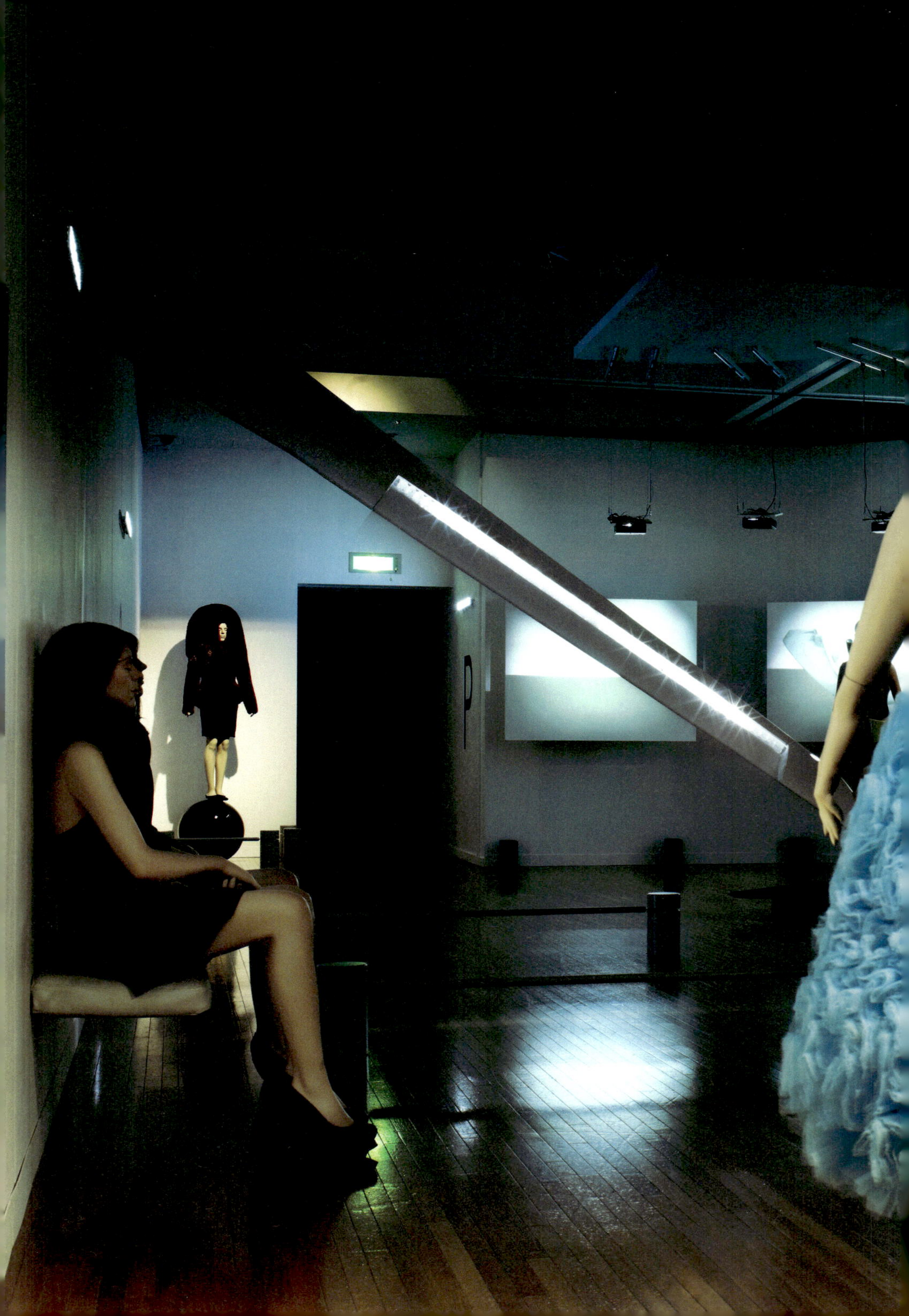

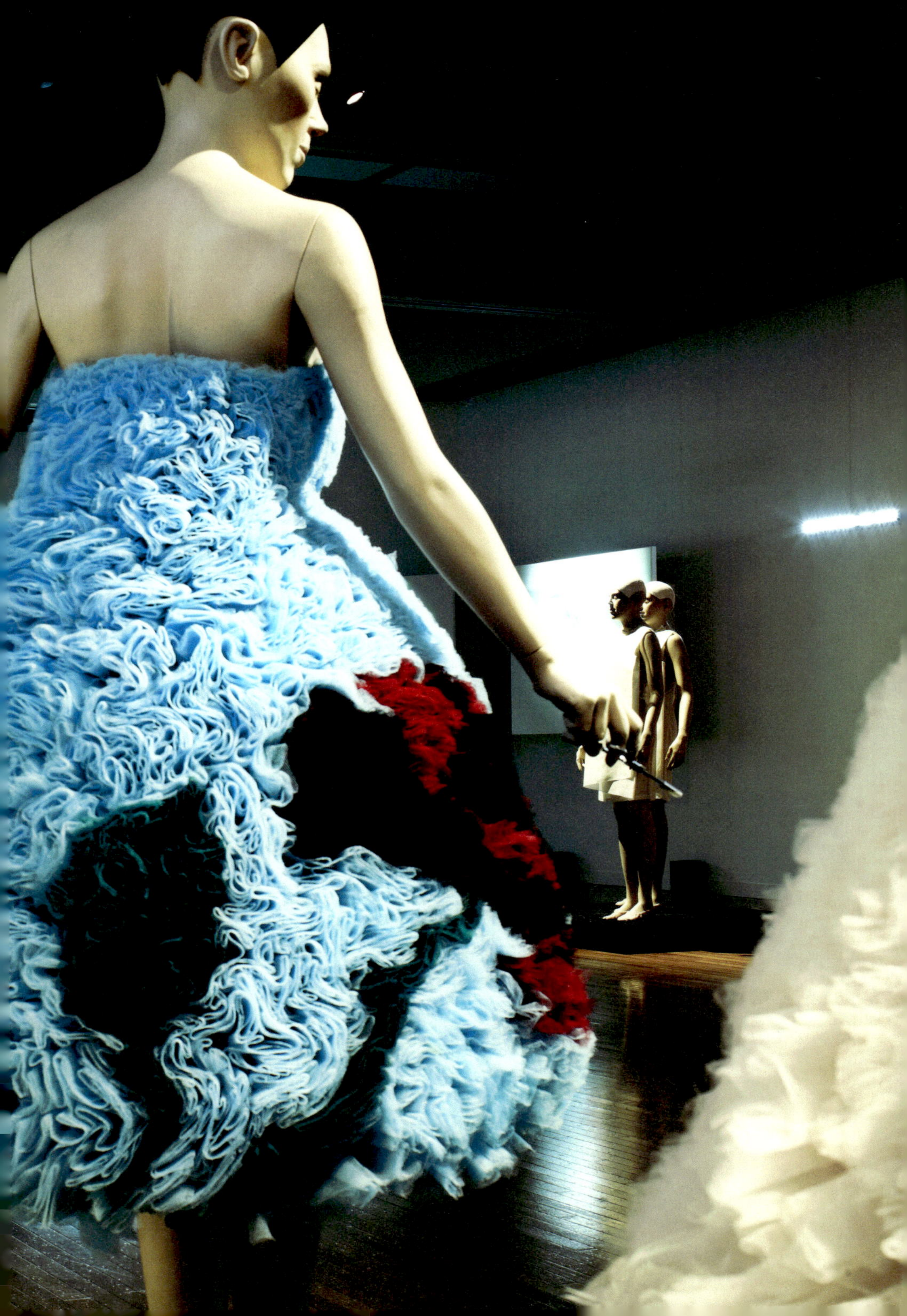

fig.

《不在の存在》| ABSENT PRESENCE (June, 2005)

2005年、チャラヤンは第51回ヴェネツィア・ビエンナーレのトルコ館代表として招かれた。この短篇映像作品は、テロリズム問題にまつわる不安感情と被害妄想を扱ったもので、入国管理の"厳格化"政策が導入されたことに起因する、外国人に対する疑念に着想を得ている。チャラヤンは、制度が将来どのように個人を尋問することになり得るのかというシナリオを描いた。ティルダ・スウィントン演じる生物学者が非英国人の女性たちに服を寄付するよう促し、その服から、彼らのDNA配列を調べるために細胞を検出する実験を行う。一連のアニメーションによって、寄付をした女性たちがどのような外見なのかが表現される。このデータは、匿名の服の提供者と実際に面接することによって、分析結果の正確性が検証されることになる。彼女たちのDNA配列は服にマッピングされ、ロンドンのサウンドスケープを構成するそれぞれ異なる音に反応する。それぞれの服は音に反応し、変形していく。その後、アクションのある時点で変形は停止し、3Dのオブジェとなる。この一連の変形過程は、どのように個人が身の回りの環境に反応するのかを表現している。

［上映時間:12分53秒］

In 2005 Chalayan was invited to represent Turkey at the 51st Venice Biennale. This short film explores the neurosis and paranoia surrounding the issue of terrorism, inspired by the introduction of 'hard line' policies on immigration and the resulting suspicion surrounding foreign individuals. Chalayan proposed a scenario depicting how institutions could in the future interrogate individuals. In an experiment, expressed as a narrative, non-British females were invited to donate clothing from which a biologist, played by the actress Tilda Swinton, extracted cells to examine their DNA sequences. A series of animations depicted how these women might look. This data was then compared to the anonymous volunteers to see how accurate the predictions were. Their DNA sequence was mapped out onto the garment and 'sensitised' to react to different sounds which make up the London soundscape. Each garment reacted and took shape accordingly. The forms seen within the animation were frozen at a point in action and transformed into 3D objects, representing how an individual reacts to their environment.
[Duration: 00:12:53]

Galerist, Istanbul   Director of Photography: Alessandra Scherillo

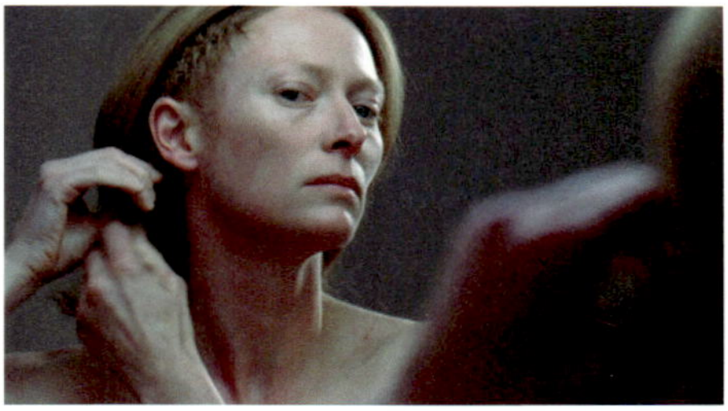
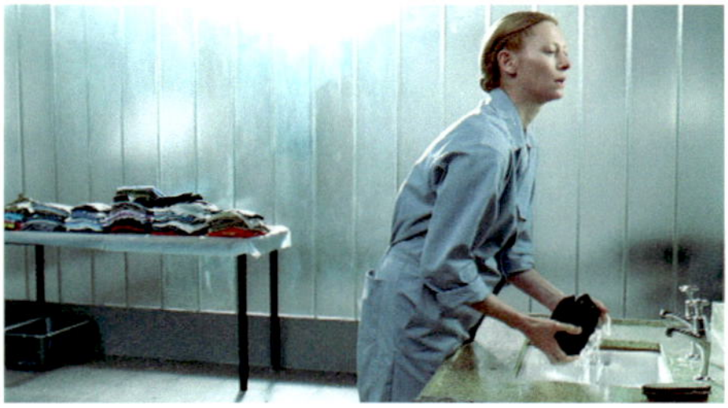
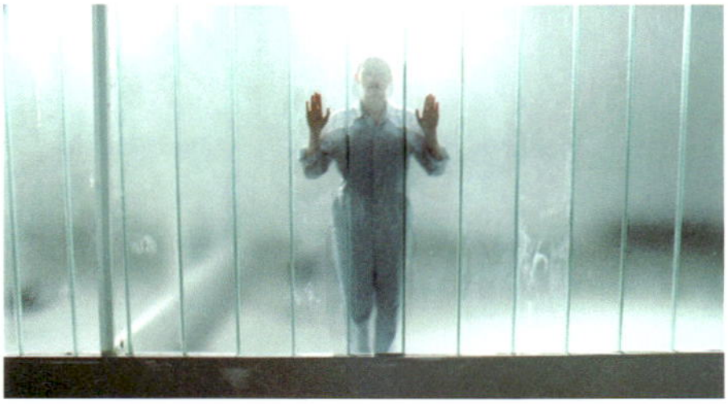
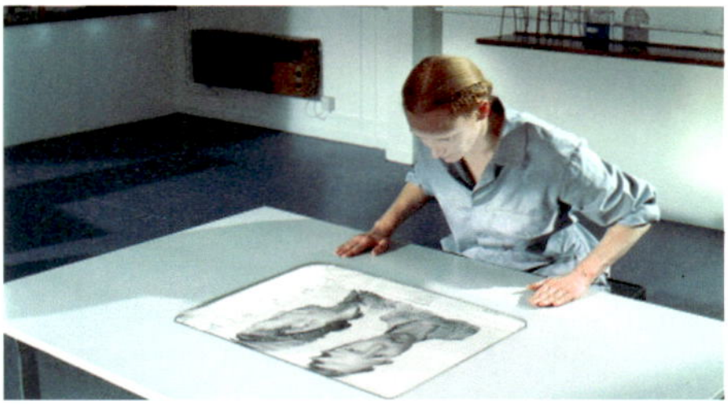
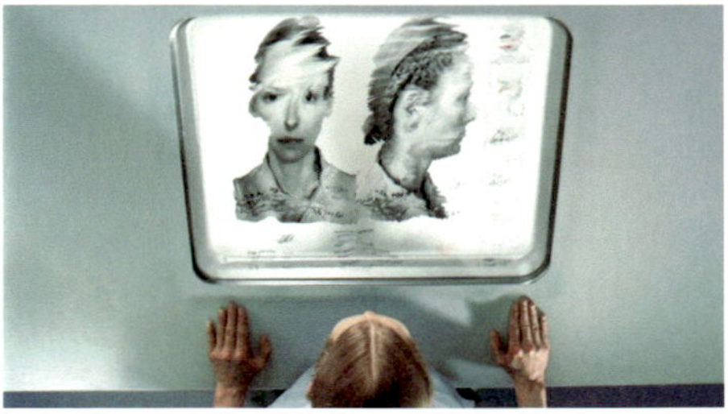
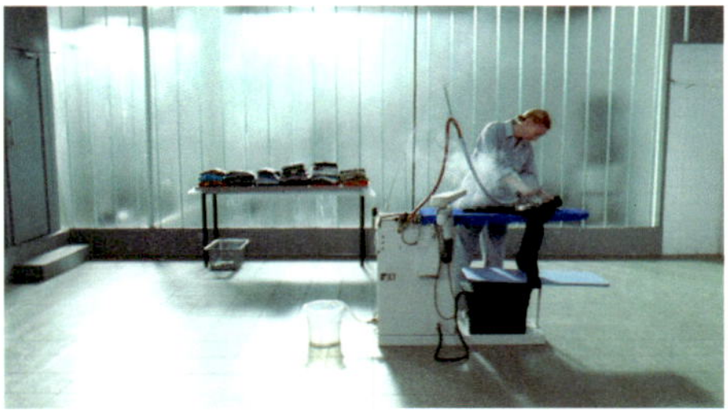
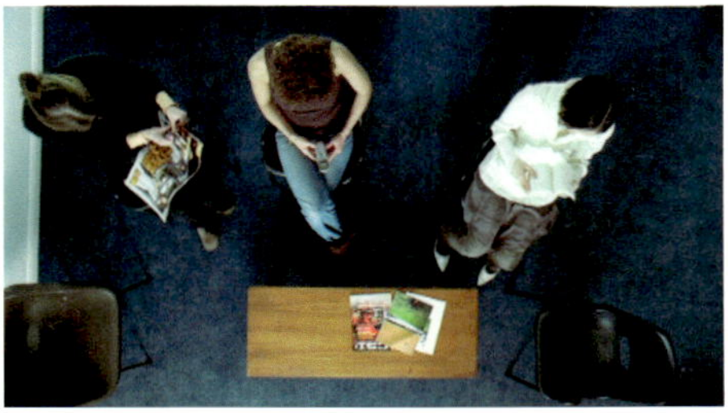
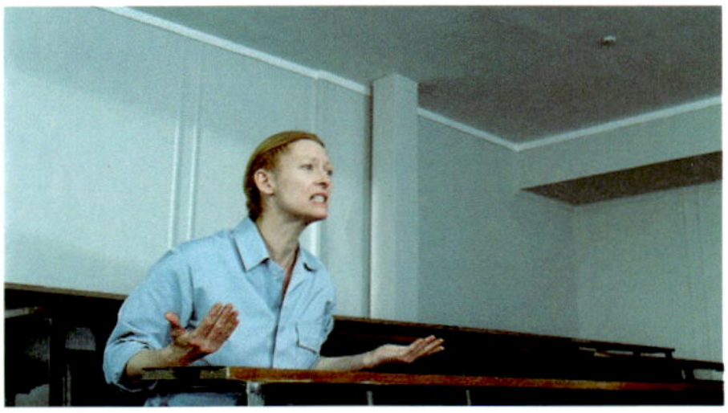
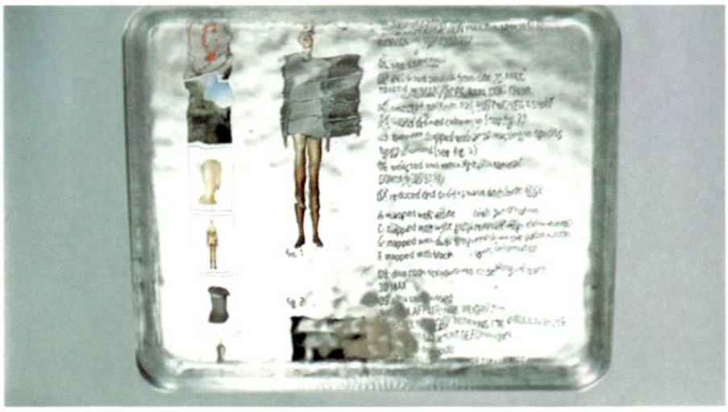
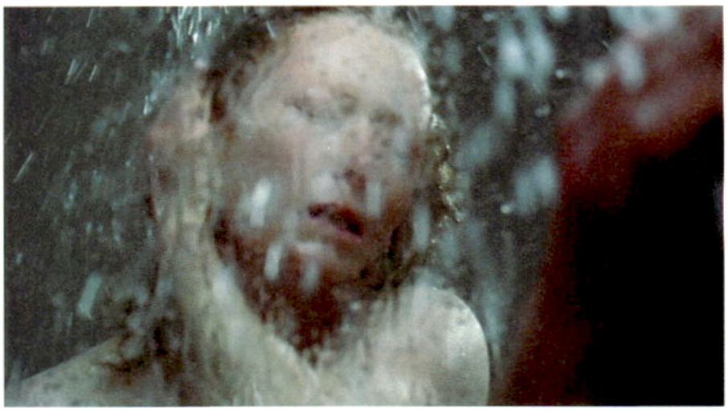

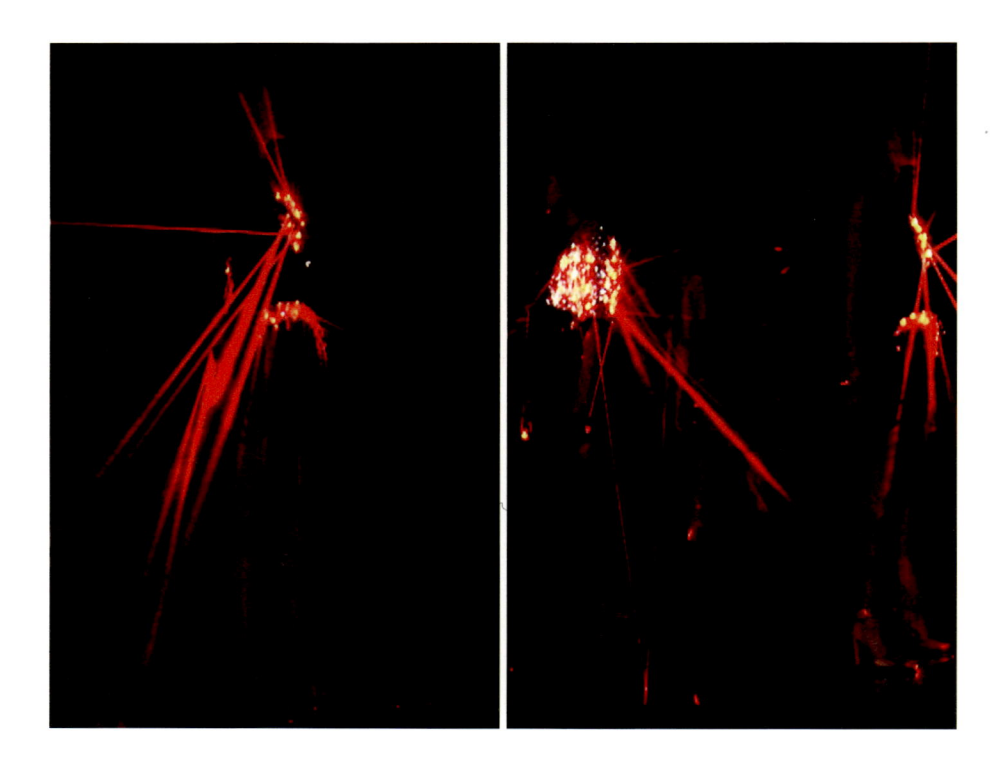

《リーディングス》 | READINGS (Spring/Summer 2008)

本コレクションは、太陽崇拝とセレブへの礼賛から着想された。本展覧会で出品されたものは、スワロフスキーのクリスタルと200本もの可動式レーザーが組み込まれたドレスに、ジャケットと帽子。この技術は、チャラヤンがここで初めて使用したもので、レーザー光線は、モーターで動くカスタムメイドの留め具で服に固定されている。最初はクリスタルの上を照らしているレーザー光線が次第に身体から離れ、何本もの赤い光線を空間に向かって解き放つ。このグラフィカルな光線は、パフォーマンスにアウラを与え、その光の空間はスペクタルの形態を創出する。

Inspired by the culture of sun worship and the cult of celebrity, the showpiece of the collection consisted of two dresses, a jacket and a hat containing Swarovski crystals and over 200 moving lasers, a technology not previously used by Chalayan. The lasers are held in place by custom-made hinges which move by motors. This trains the lasers first on the crystals before moving away from the body creating a matrix of red laser light. The graphical rays represent the aura of performance, with the light space becoming an alternative form of spectacle.

Dress, jacket: Swarovksi, London   Dress and laser hat: Han Nefkins

fig. J

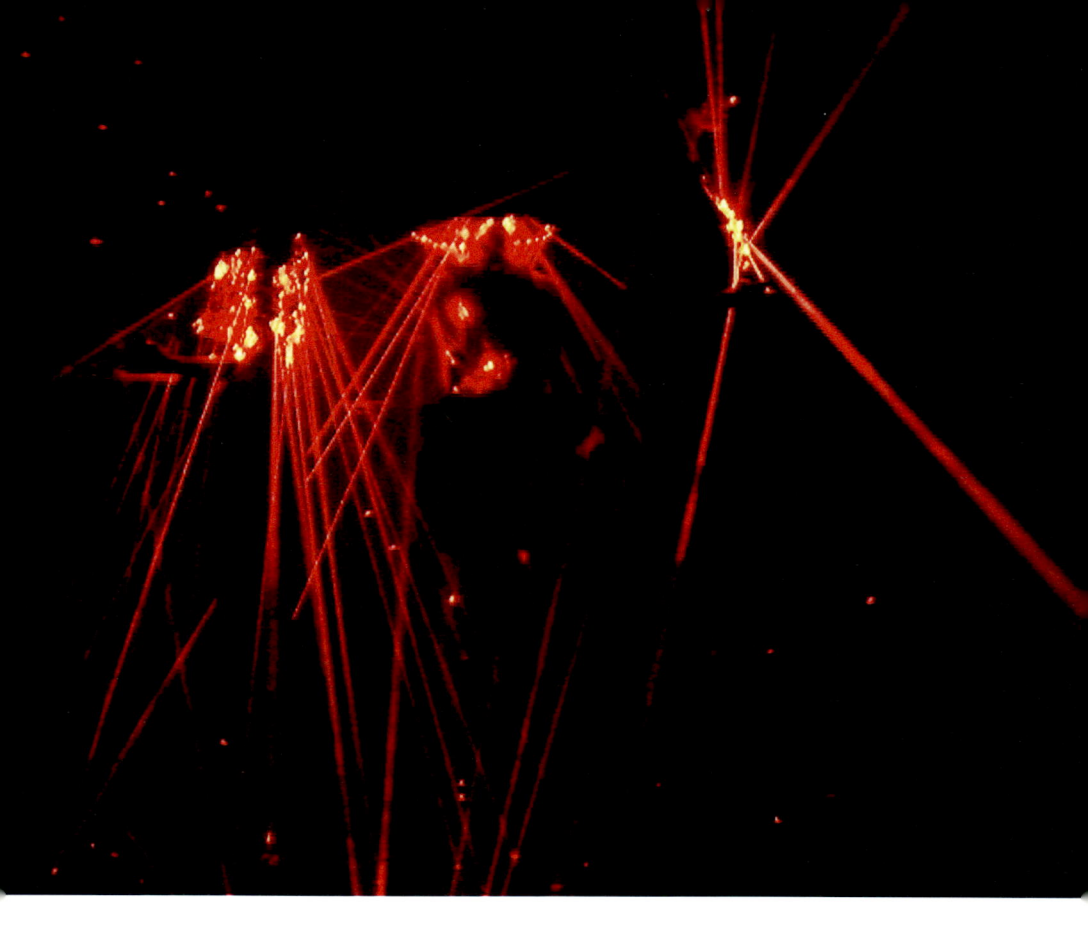

《ビフォア・マイナス・ナウ》
BEFORE MINUS NOW (Spring/Summer 2000)

《ビフォア・マイナス・ナウ》は人類、テクノロジー、そして自然の力の関係を探究した作品である。インスピレーションの源となったものは重力、膨張、天候といった無形の現象——つまりそれらは、自然界に多様な形状を生み出す力である。重力は古典的な赤いフレアドレスによって喚起させられる。合金と電力によってこのドレスは広がり、変形する。またもう一つのセクションは、山々が何世紀にもおよぶ地殻変動の突き上げや浸食によって形成された過程に着想を得ている。このセクションでチャラヤンは不定形のチュールの層を、標準的なドレスの形状に近づけるために長さに違いをつけてカットした。フィナーレは炭素繊維でできたリモート・コントロール・ドレスであり、人工的な力によってボディの形状が変えられるというものであった。ショーでは、1人の少年がキャットウォークに登場し、この合成繊維のドレスをリモコンで"操作"し、ドレスの後部パネルを開けて内側の柔らかなチュールを露にさせた。人間をシンプルなリモコンで操作するというアイデアによって、生命をコントロールしたいという人間の性向と、テクノロジーへの私たちの過度な期待をやんわりと批判している。

Before Minus Now explored the relationship between mankind, technology and natural forces. The sources of inspiration were intangible phenomena such as gravity, expansion and the weather - forces which cause many different shapes in nature. Gravity was evoked by a classical, red flaring dress in which memory alloy and electricity enabled the dress to expand and change shape. Another section was inspired by the way in which mountains are created by centuries of tectonic thrust and erosion. For this, Chalayan used a shapeless bale of tulle that was cut away gradually in order to arrive at a more regular dress shape. The finale was a carbon fibre Remote Control Dress which transformed the body through an artificial man-made force. During the presentation a boy came onto the catwalk to 'operate' the synthetic dress with a remote control which opened up the panels of the dress to reveal the soft tulle inside. The idea of directing human beings with a simple remote control system is a light-hearted reflection on the human tendency to want to control life, as well as our exaggerated expectations of technology.

fig. **K**

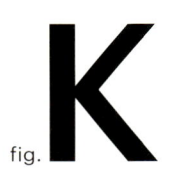

fig. **L**

《明白なる運命》| MANIFEST DESTINY (Spring/Summer 2003)

チャラヤンは西洋の拡張主義の物理的、心理的な影響に関心を寄せている。厳密な西洋の服のスタンダード、例えばしばしば身体を覆い隠し、紐で編み上げ、変形させようとするような規格は、そうしたイデオロギーを押しつけるための手段と見なすことができる。チャラヤンはこのコレクションにおいて先進国における服の意味を探り、西洋の伝統から身体を解放することを試みた。手始めに解剖学に基づいて服をデザインし、服の下にある身体を露呈させるために弾力性のあるストレッチ素材を用いた。最後の4着のドレスには様々な箇所に穴を開け、身体の諸器官をあらわし、また色のついたストライプは重なり合った皮膚の層を表現している。

Chalayan is interested in the physical and psychological results of Western expansionism. Strict Western clothing standards can be perceived as a means of imposing such ideologies, which often seek to cover, lace-up and deform the body. Chalayan used the collection to explore the meaning of clothes in the developed world and to liberate the body from Western traditions. He designed clothes with the anatomy as the starting point, revealed by the elasticity of the materials used to reveal the body beneath. The final four dresses bore holes cut in different areas representing the organs of the body and coloured strips representing various layers of skin.

Collection: Musee d'Art Moderne Grand-Duc Jean, Mudam Luxembourg;
Collection: Groninger Museum, Groningen

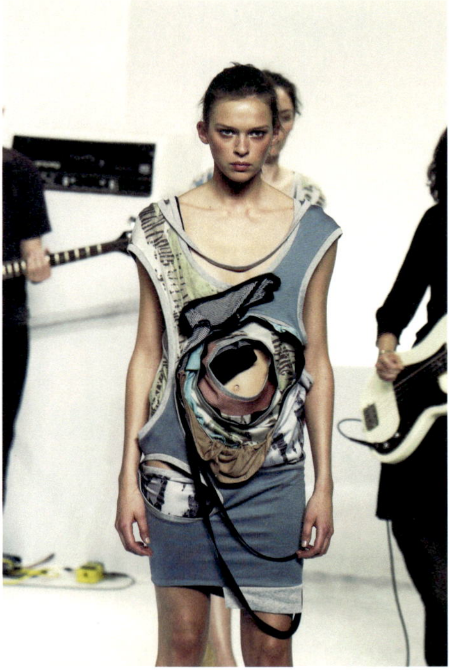

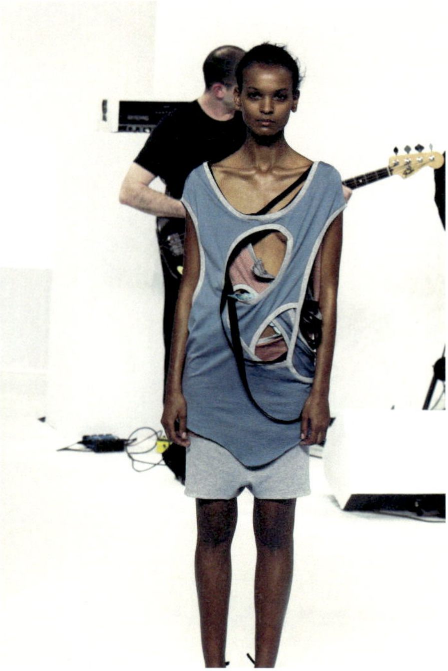

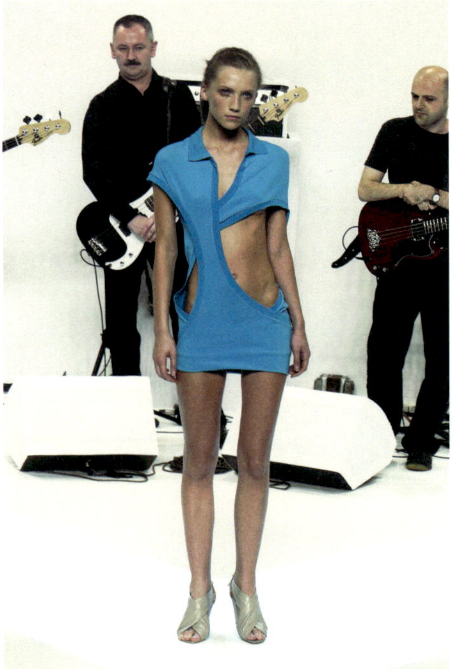

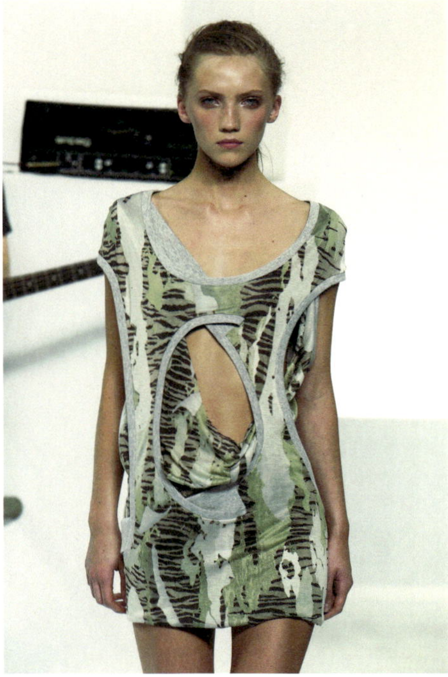

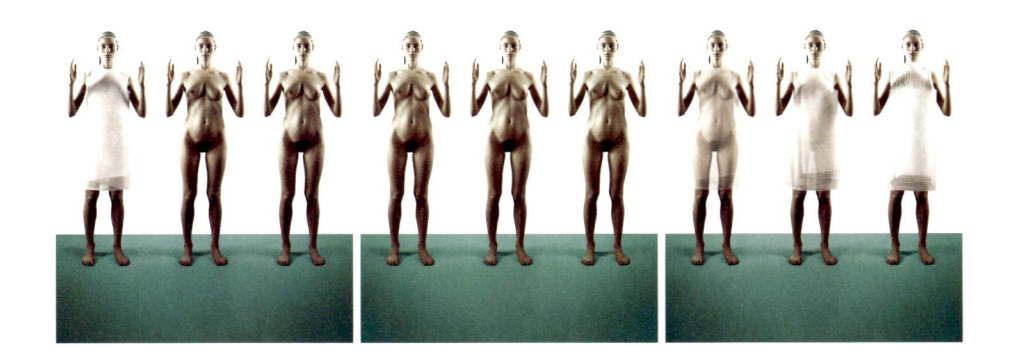

《ジオトロピクス（屈地性研究）》| GEOTROPICS (Spring/Summer 1999)

《ジオトロピクス》では、戦争や文化をもたらす、国境や河といった地勢的な特徴がもつ役割を考察する。チャラヤンは、中国から西洋へと続く2000年もの歴史を有するシルクロードに沿って、異なる時代と場所の民族衣装を混在させたCGアニメーションによって、身体のいわばマイクロ地理学を生み出した。次から次へと変化する服によって旅を表現し、時を超えたシルクロードの旅を表現するアニメーションが誕生した。片側の襟は見えているのに反対側は消えているといった個々の服は、場所から場所へと移動する結果として生じるものである。このショーのフィナーレは記念碑的なドレス2着で構成された。その内の一つは椅子と一体化した服で、モデルと椅子が単体の存在に見えるものだった。

Geotropics reflects upon the role of topographical features such as borders and rivers in shaping wars and cultures. Chalayan created a microgeography of the body in a computer animation that fused together national costumes from different dates and places along the 2,000 year old Silk Road from China to the West. The animation became the idea of a journey through time and the Silk Road, with garments morphing into one another, used to represent the journey. Articles of clothing were generated as a result of moving from one place to another, where a piece of collar was visible on one side but had disappeared on the other. The show's finale was formed by two monumental dresses, one of which was a chair integrated into a garment so that the model and chair appeared to be a single entity.

fig. M

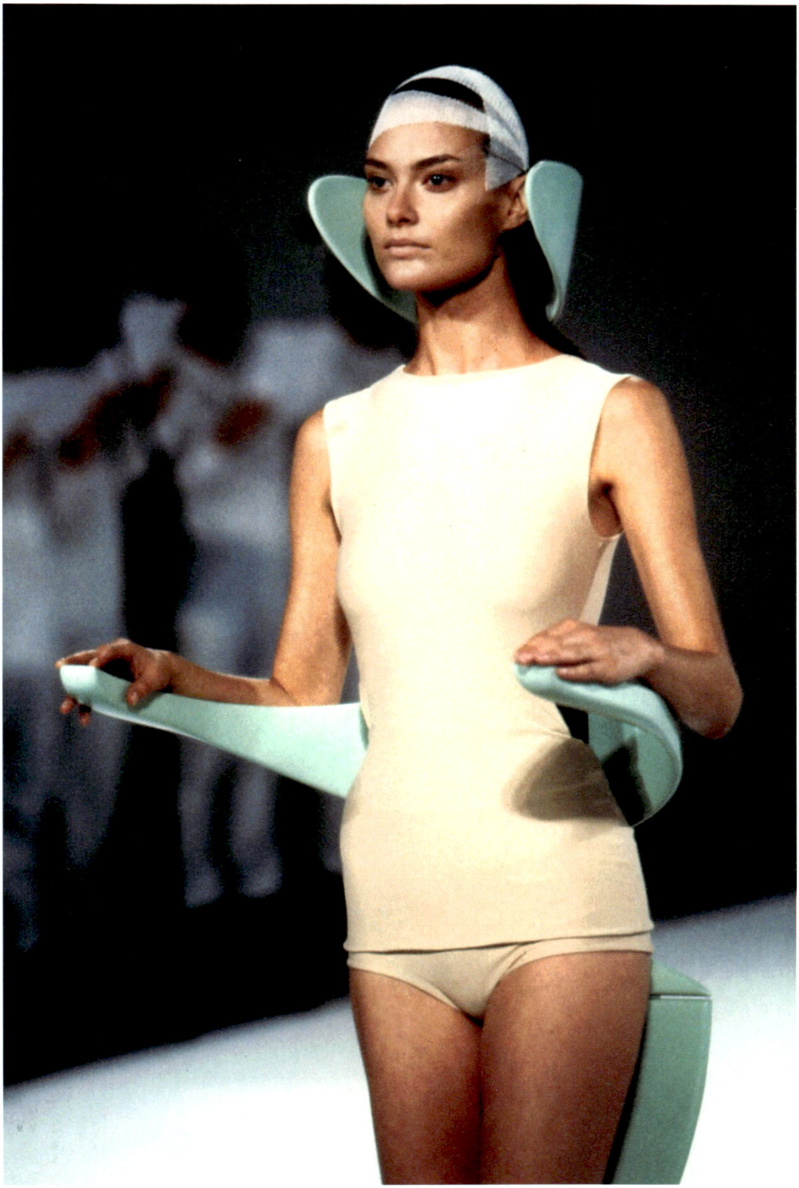

《休息》| REPOSE (Autumn/Winter 2006)

チャラヤンは空を飛ぶという概念に魅了されている。彼は空港を国境と見なしているると同時に、自身のトルコ系キプロス人としての立場とロンドンでの生活との文化的な隔たりを象徴する、物理的な境界であるとも捉えている。《休息》は2006年、クンストハレ・マンハイムのクリスタル・パレスのために、スワロフスキーの依頼によって制作されたインスタレーション作品である。航空機の翼が壁から突き出し、大きなフラップがゆっくりと上下すると、後方からずらりと並ぶLEDライトによって、スワロフスキーのクリスタルが照らし出されるという仕掛けである。また1人掛け用の椅子も壁から突き出しているため、乗客は航空機の外に座っていることになり、このことは、飛行が身体感覚からかけ離れた経験であることを明示しながら、空を飛ぶことの不条理さや興奮、そしてその体験を表現している。《休息》は後に、イスタンブール・モダンが購入し、現在は常設展示されている。

*デジタル時計には特別仕様カットのクリスタル、24個のLEDライトと96個の八角形のクリスタルを使用している。

Chalayan is fascinated by the concept of flight. He views airports as borders, and the physical divide in between symbolically representing the cultural divide between his own Turkish Cypriot heritage and his life in London. Repose is a conceptual art installation originally commissioned by Swarovski for their Crystal Palace installation at Kunstalle Mannheim in 2006. An aircraft wing protrudes from the wall, its large flap moving slowly up and down to reveal a long strip of Swarovski crystals illuminated from behind by LED lights. A single seat folding out from the wall, with a passenger sitting outside the aircraft, represents absurdity, excitement and experience of flying, manifesting itself as an out of body experience. A version of Repose was later purchased by Istanbul Modern where it is now on permanent display.

Digital clock featuring specially cut crystals, LED strip of light featuring 24 LEDs and 96 crystal octagons. Swarovski, Crystal Palace

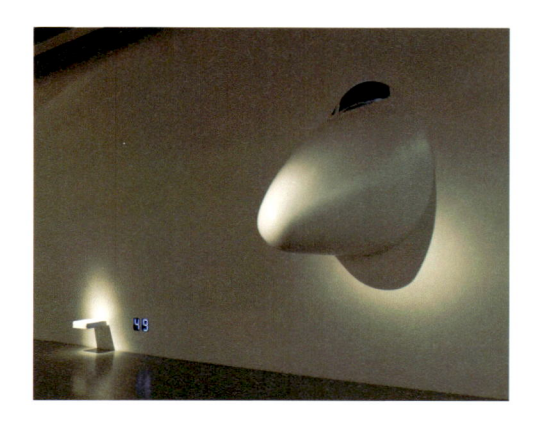

fig. N

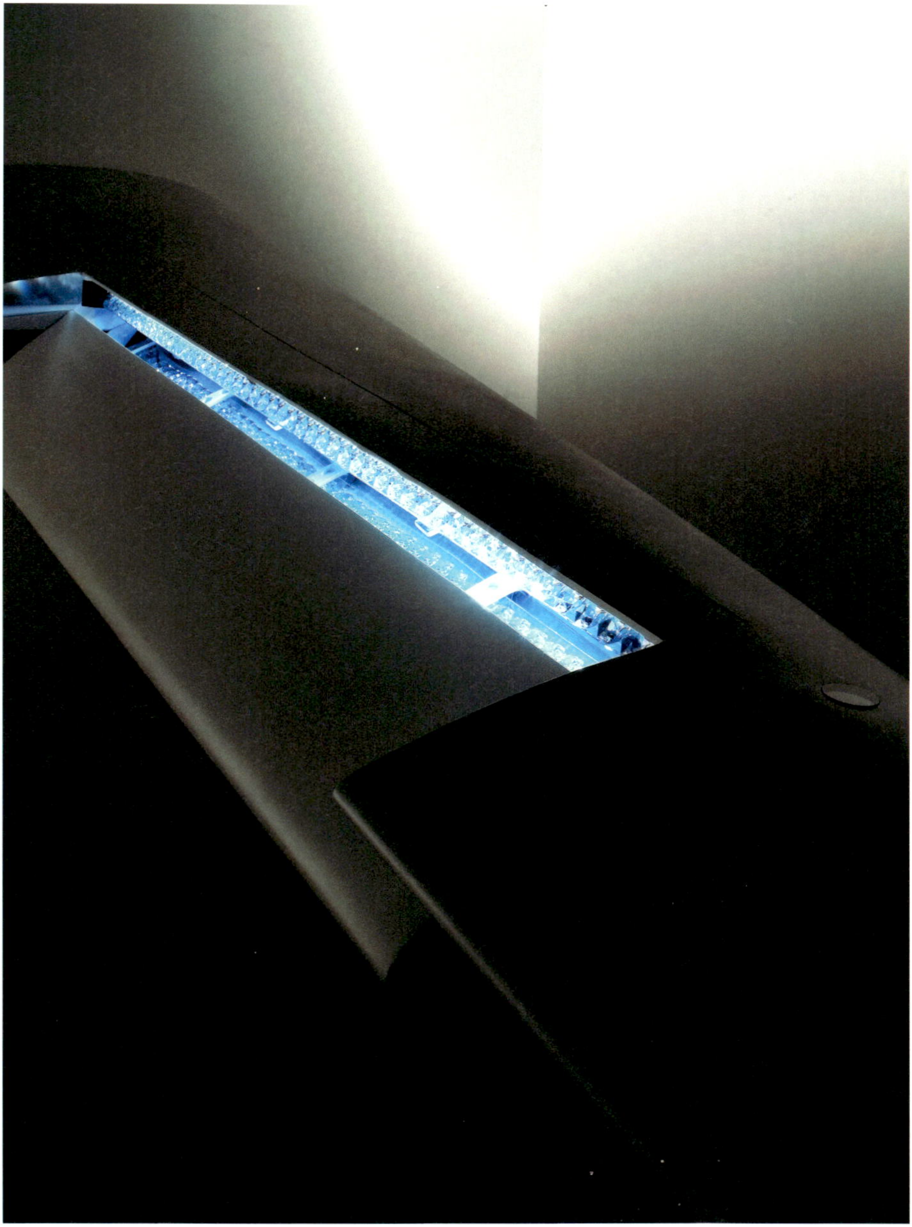

《場から旅路へ》| PLACE TO PASSAGE (October, 2003)

《場から旅路へ》は、チャラヤンがデジタル・デザイナーのニュートラルとのコラボレーションによって発案、監督した短篇映像作品である。この映像は私たちの意識にあるスピード、テクノロジー、移動が意味するものを、幾つものメタファーやシンボルを使って探究したもの。このプロジェクトはチャラヤンがレーシングカーのファンタジーを構想したことから始まった。B.A.R.ホンダ・レーシングF1チームを訪れたことで着想を得たチャラヤンは、同じモデリングの技術を使って流線形のポッド(蚕のまゆ)型の構造物を造り、これを5スクリーンのインスタレーションの中心とした。ロンドンからイスタンブールへの想像の旅を生み出し、観る者をリアルな都会のストリートから夢のような風景へといざなう。スピードを上げるポッドには中性的な女性が乗っており、彼女はその中に、一時避難所、もう一つの人生の記憶、孤独、郷愁、探検といったものがすべて一つに混ざり合っている架空の生活空間を作り出している。ポッドの最後の旅はボスポラス海峡である。ポッドが最後に地下の駐車場へ入っていく前に、イスタンブールの街の中央に位置し、アジア側とヨーロッパ側を隔てている、この海峡を通る。これが旅の終点であると同時に、新たな旅路の出発点でもあることを象徴的に表している。

[上映時間:12分40秒]

The film explores the implications of speed, technology and displacement on our psyche by using a number of metaphors and symbols which hint at the idea of displacement. The project began with Chalayan creating his own fantasy vision of a racing car. Inspired by a visit to the B.A.R. Honda Formula One racing team, Chalayan used the same modelling techniques to build an aerodynamic pod-like structure which became the centre piece of the five-screen installation. He created an imagined journey from London to Istanbul that takes the viewer through raw urban streets to a dreamlike landscape. The speeding pod carries an androgynous female passenger who has created an imaginary living space where temporary refuge, memories of another life, isolation, nostalgia and exploration all merge into one. The pod's final journey is along the Bosphorus, the river running through the centre of the city of Istanbul which marks the division between Asia and Europe, before finally docking in an underground car park that symbolically marks both the end, and the start, of a new journey.
[Duration: 00.12.40]

Hussein Chalayan Multi-screen installation, 2003
Curated by Artwise Curators / A Tribe Art Commission   Music by Jean Paul Dessy
Post production, 3D animation, special effects and editing by Neutral.

fig. O

49

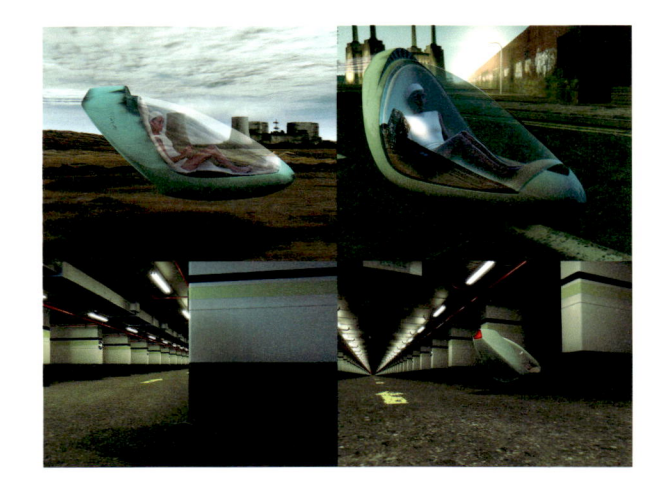

P
fig.

《ゲノメトリクス（ゲノム測定）》 | GENOMETRICS (Autumn/Winter 2005)

ロンドンに暮らす異なる背景をもつ人々を対象に、彼らのDNA配列がロンドンのサウンドスケープにどのような影響を受け、その結果、どのようにこの街に適応しているのかを考察した作品である。ここでは、特別に開発されたプログラムが使用され、彼らのDNA配列の各文字は服の上にマッピングされ、それが街のサウンドスケープを構成する音に反応していく。この一連のプログラムから生まれた多様な形態は、街の音に反応していく過程がピークに達した時点で静止したものであり、それが本コレクションのデザインのベースとなっている。

Like Absent Presence, Genometrics evolved from the idea of how different individuals living in London would fit into London life depending on the reaction of their DNA sequences to the London soundscape through a specifically developed programme. Each letter of their DNA sequence was mapped out on the garment and 'sensitised' to react to different sounds which make up the soundscape. The shapes seen within the animation were frozen at a peak point in action creating the basis for design.

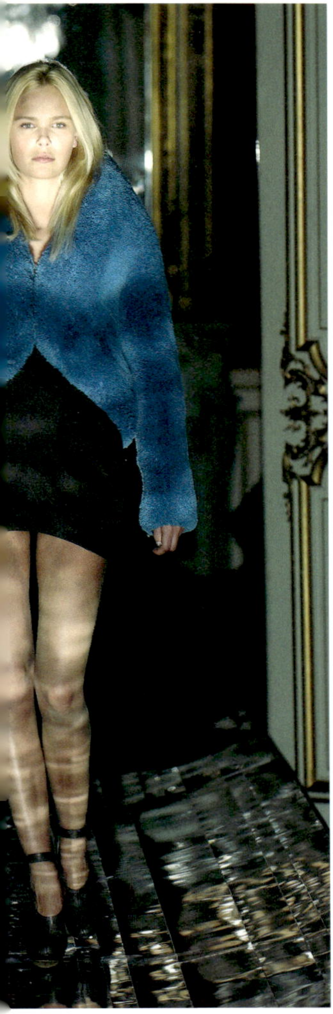

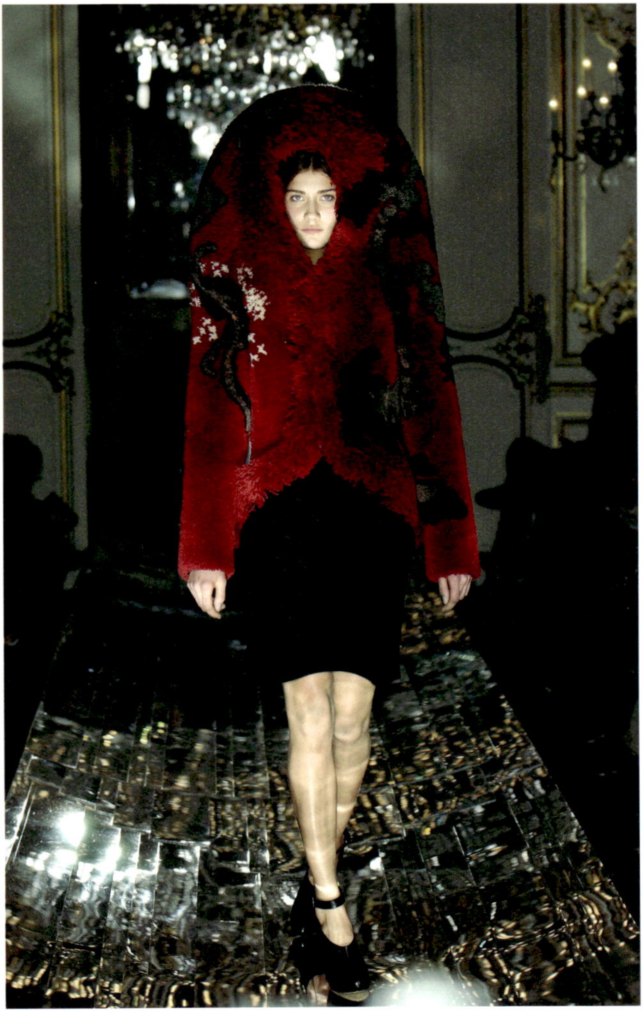

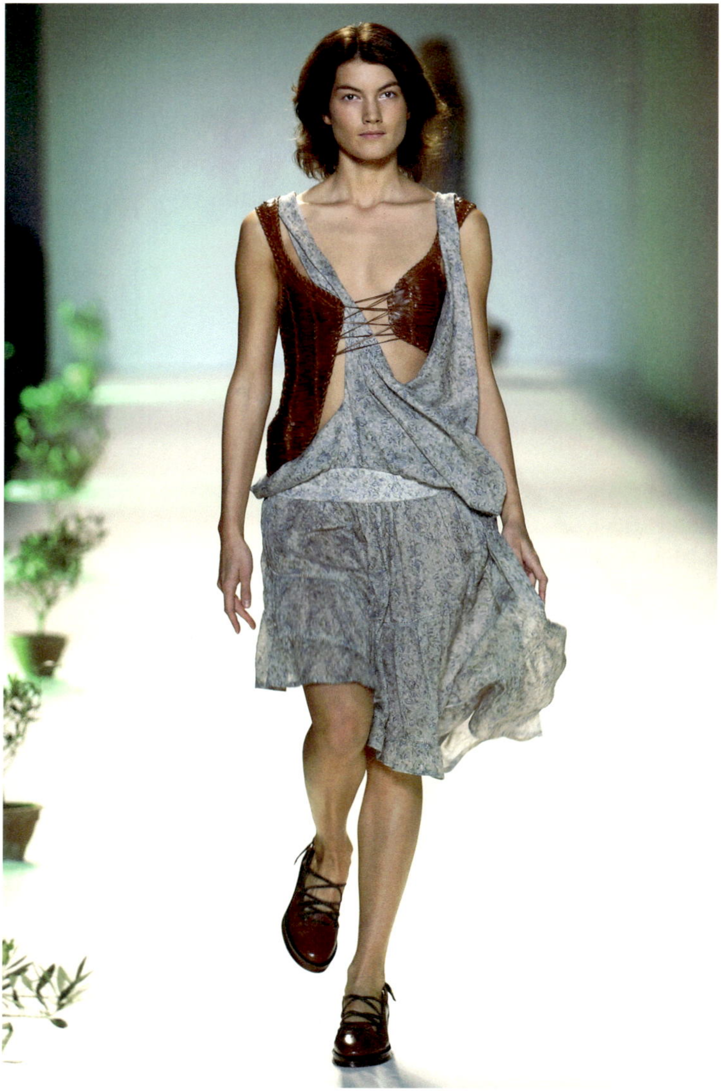
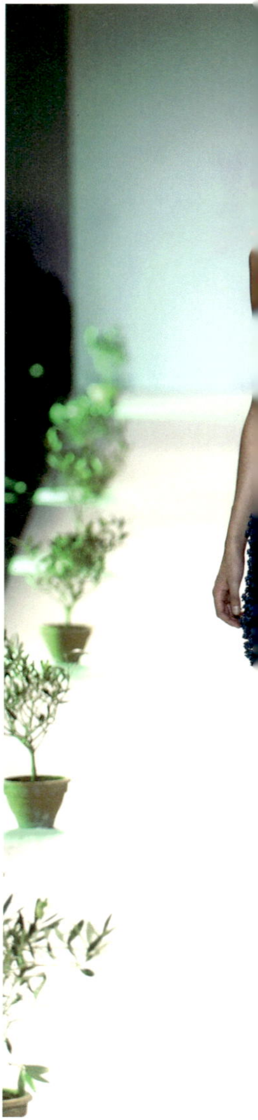

fig. **Q**

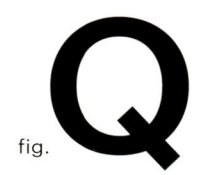

《ブラインドスケープ》 | BLINDSCAPE, (Spring/Summer 2005)

盲目になるとは、どのような感じであろうか？それが《ブラインドスケープ》というコレクションの始まりだった。チャラヤンは目隠しをして、ジャケットやパンツといったごく基本的なアイテムのスケッチを行った。ショーでは、悪夢を象徴する獰猛なモンスターで溢れる荒れ狂う海が描かれた、野性的で劇的なプリントの服が発表された。最後は、穏やかな海に入り、青いビーズをあしらい、静かな海をあらわしたプリント柄の服でショーを締めくくった。東京都現代美術館のインスタレーションでは、7つの島の上でそれぞれマネキンがオリーブの木に水をやり、彼の子供時代の心象風景でもあるキプロス島の情景を描き出した。

What is it like to be blind? It was from this question that he embarked on the challenging collection Blindscape. Chalayan blindfolded himself and drew designs of very basic items such as jackets and trousers. In the show, some wild, dramatic prints of stormy sea, full of fierce monsters symbolizing a nightmare, were shown. The show was concluded as the sea calmed down, with prints representing tranquil sea and blue beads. This installation was created by Chalayan especially for the Design Museum Tank. In the installation at the Museum of Contemporary Art Tokyo, a mannequin watered olive trees on each of seven islands, creating the Mediterranean atmosphere of Northern Cyprus, which is also imagined scenery of his childhood.

Collection: Groninger Museum, Groningen

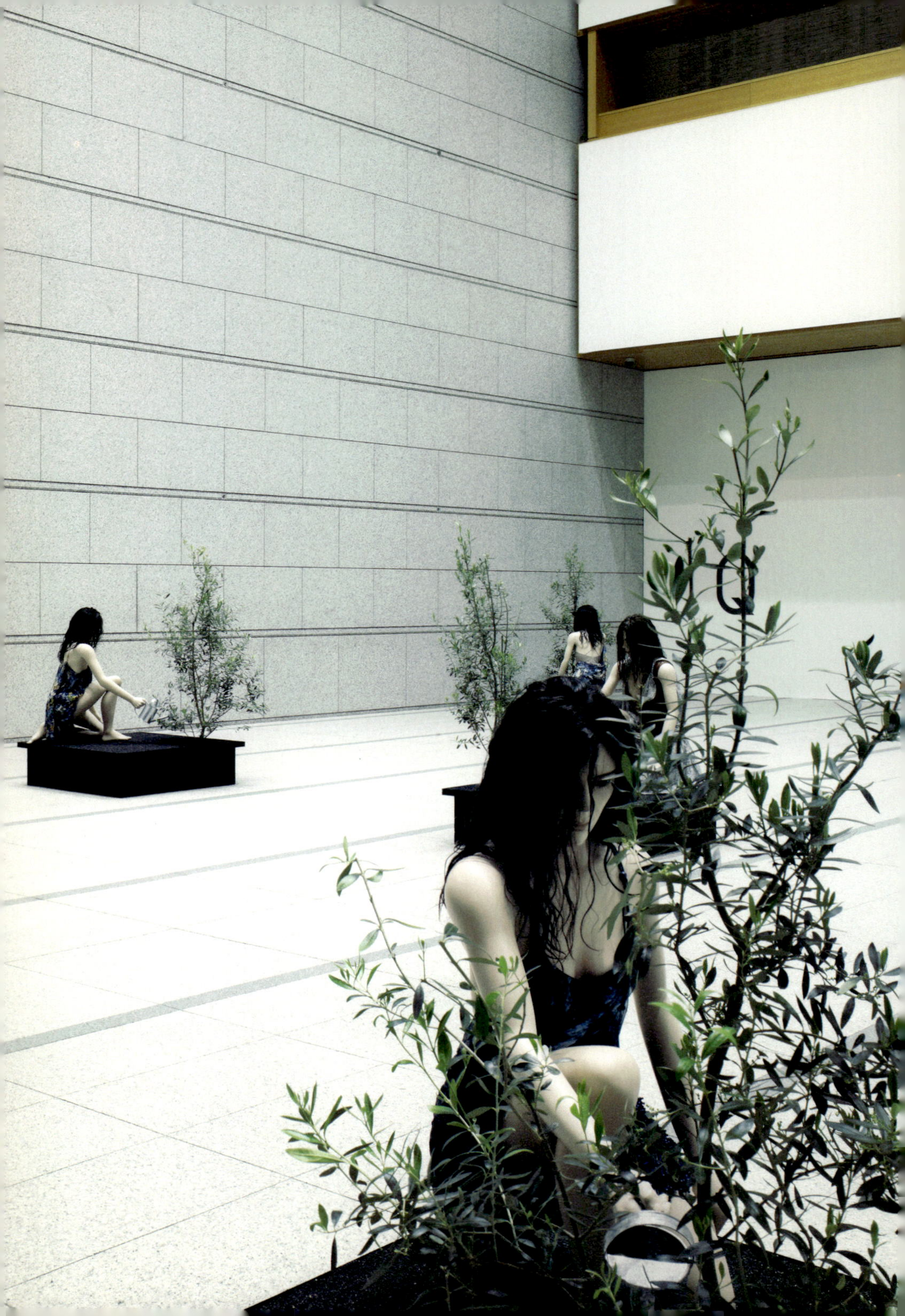

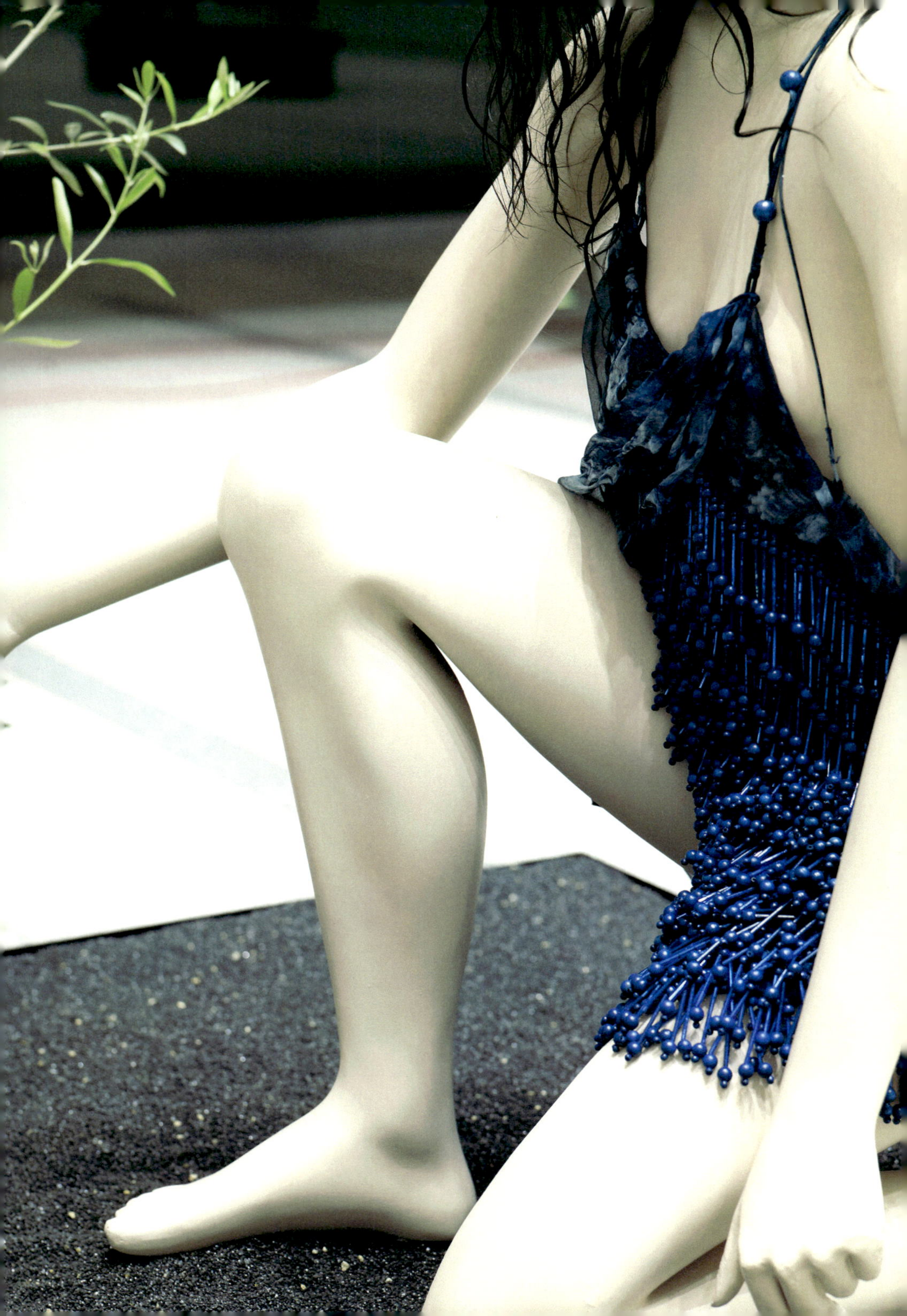

fig. **R**

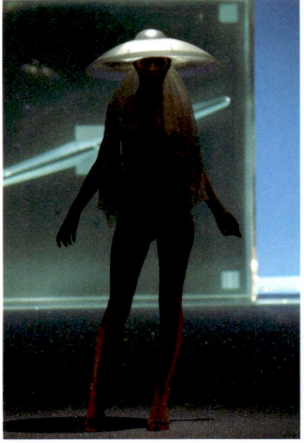

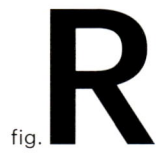

《111》| ONE HUNDRED AND ELEVEN (Spring/Summer 2007)

本コレクションは、ここ111年の間に起こった戦争や革命、あるいは政治的、社会的変化を含む様々な出来事に影響を受けながら、ファッションがどのうように変遷してきたかを探求している。これらの変化は、服を厳密な時系列に沿って並べることで表現されている。最後には、部分的に動くメカニカルドレスのシリーズが登場し、ある時代のスタイルから次の時代のスタイルへと、抽象的に形を変えていく様を表現した。

This collection explored how fashion has been shaped by the events of the last one hundred and eleven years, including wars, revolutions, political and social changes. These changes were represented by clothing shown in strict historical chronological order. They were finally shown by a series of mechanical dresses which, as parts moved, abstractly morphed from one era's style to another.

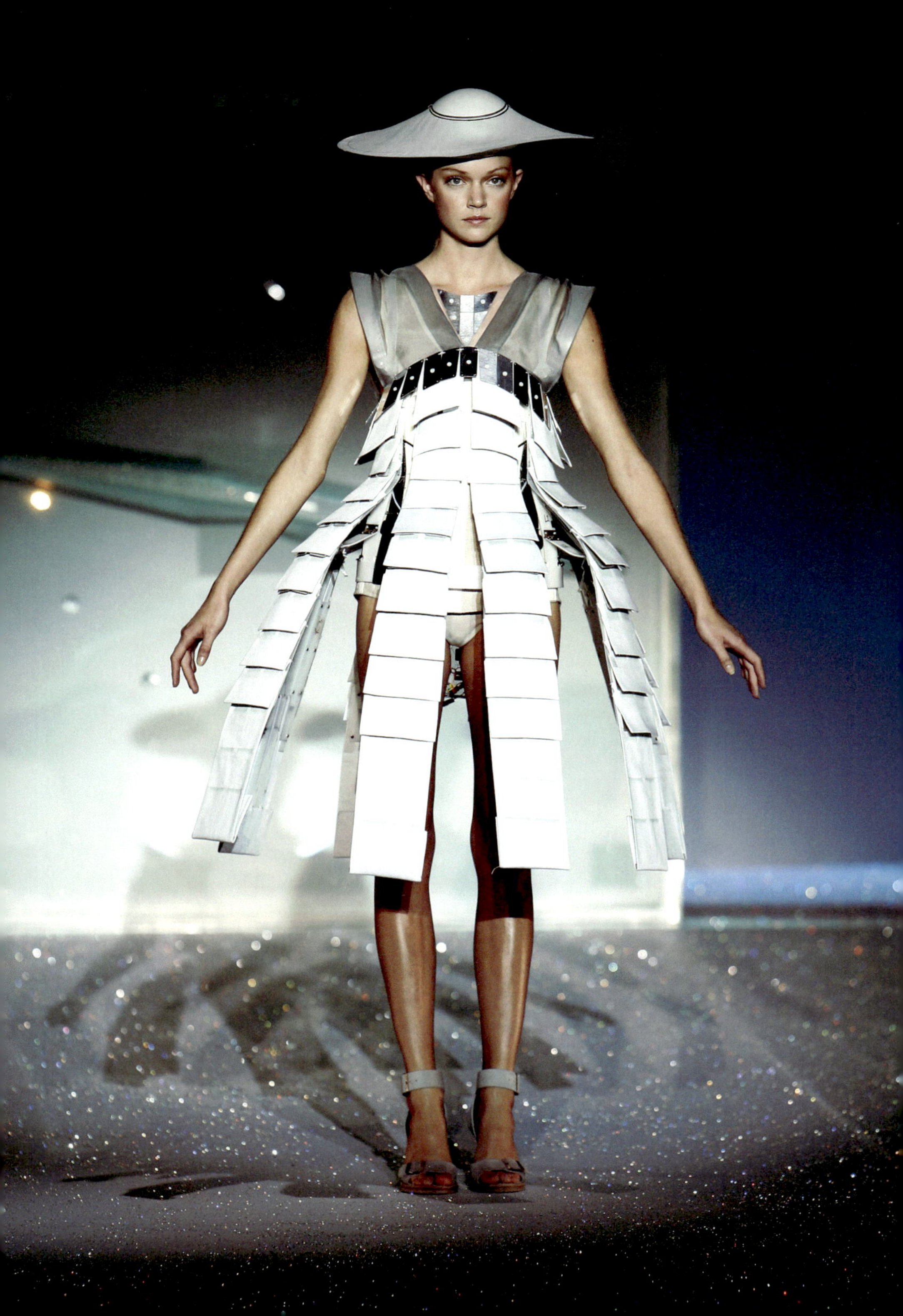

麻酔 | ANAESTHETICS, 2004

本作品は11の場面から構成され、各シーンは儀式的なものや私たちのふるまいを制御するコードの中にいかに暴力性が潜んでいるかを示している。例えば、きれいに盛りつけられた刺身。主人公は、料理人によって生きた魚がさばかれていく光景を目にすることなく、その刺身を食す。また、目隠しをされた子供が笑いながら銃を構える様や整形手術、結婚、飛行機の旅、記念写真など、チャラヤンが自身の経験の中で目にした暴力性をまるでスケッチブックに書き留めるかのように、それぞれのシーンが展開していく。
［上映時間：22分22秒］

This work consists of 11 scenes, each of which reveals hidden violence in ceremonies or codes that control our behaviours. For example, an elegant assortment of sashimi is eaten by the protagonist who never sees the chef cutting up living fish. A blindfolded laughing child who readies a gun, a cosmetic surgery, a marriage, inside the aircraft, souvenir photography, and other scenes are randomly presented; as if Chalayan has compiled a sketchbook of violent episodes.
[Duration: 00:22:22]

fig. S

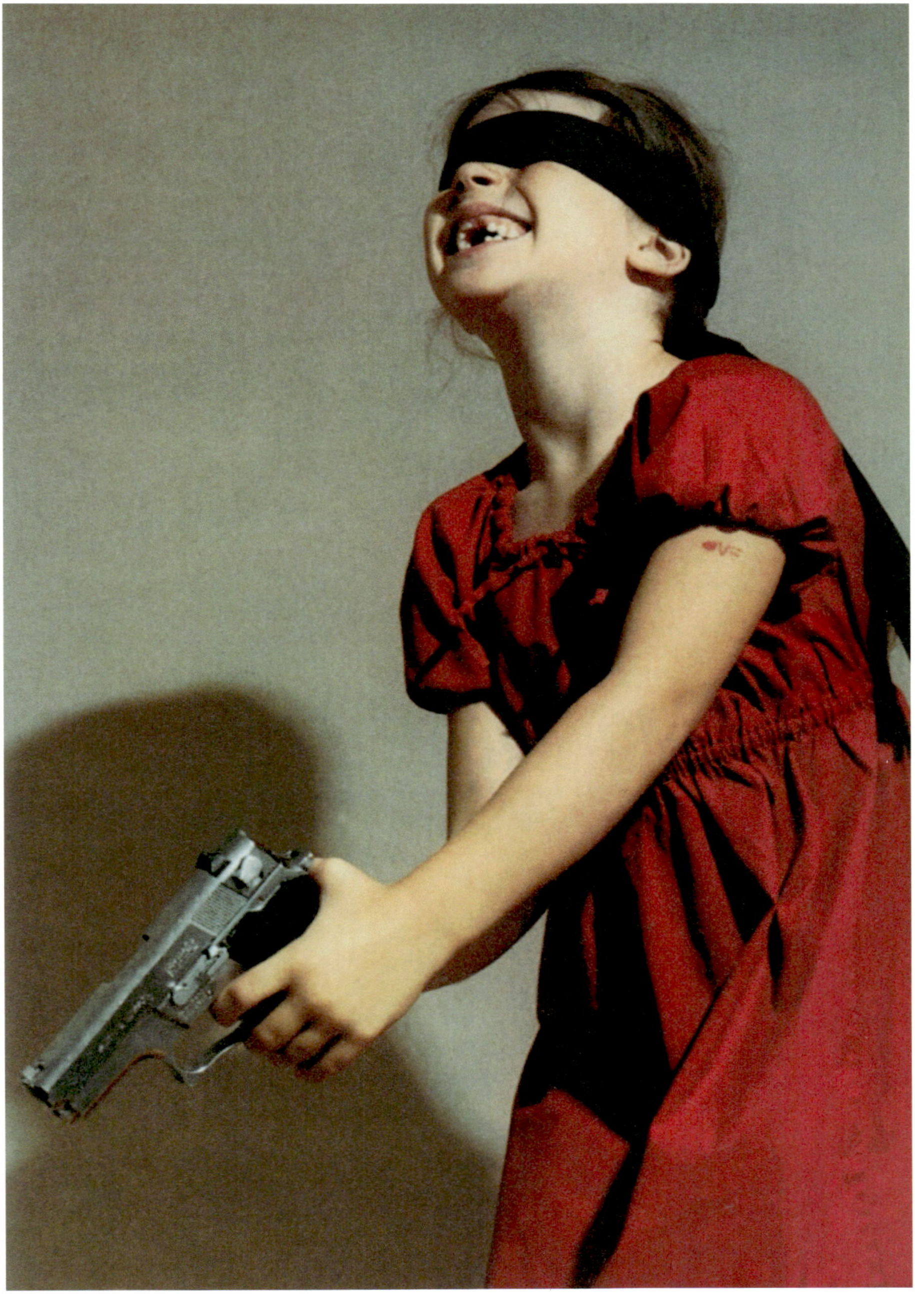

fig. T

《エアボーン》| AIRBORNE (Autumn/Winter 2007)

私たちの文化は、死とは生と相反する力であると見なす世界観を確立してきた。世界の多様な気候をメタファーとして使用したこのコレクションは、天候のサイクルとリンクするある種の力や死への恐怖を反映させている。気候は絶えず移り変わり、あらゆる生命体の生と死は、つねに流動的な状態であることを示している。このプロジェクトは春、夏、秋、冬の、4つのパートで構成された、春と夏のパートでは、それぞれ1万5600個のLEDとクリスタルを組み合わせたLEDドレスが発表された。

Our culture has established a world view where death is seen as an opposite force to life. Using world climates as a metaphor, this collection reflects upon our sense of empowerment and our fears of mortality linked to weather cycles. The climate constantly renews and recreates, demonstrating that the life and death of all life forms are in a constant state of flux. The project was presented in four parts - Spring, Summer, Autumn and Winter. Spring and Summer each featured an extraordinary LED dress consisting of 15,600 LEDS combined with crystal displays.

LED Dress: Swarovski, London

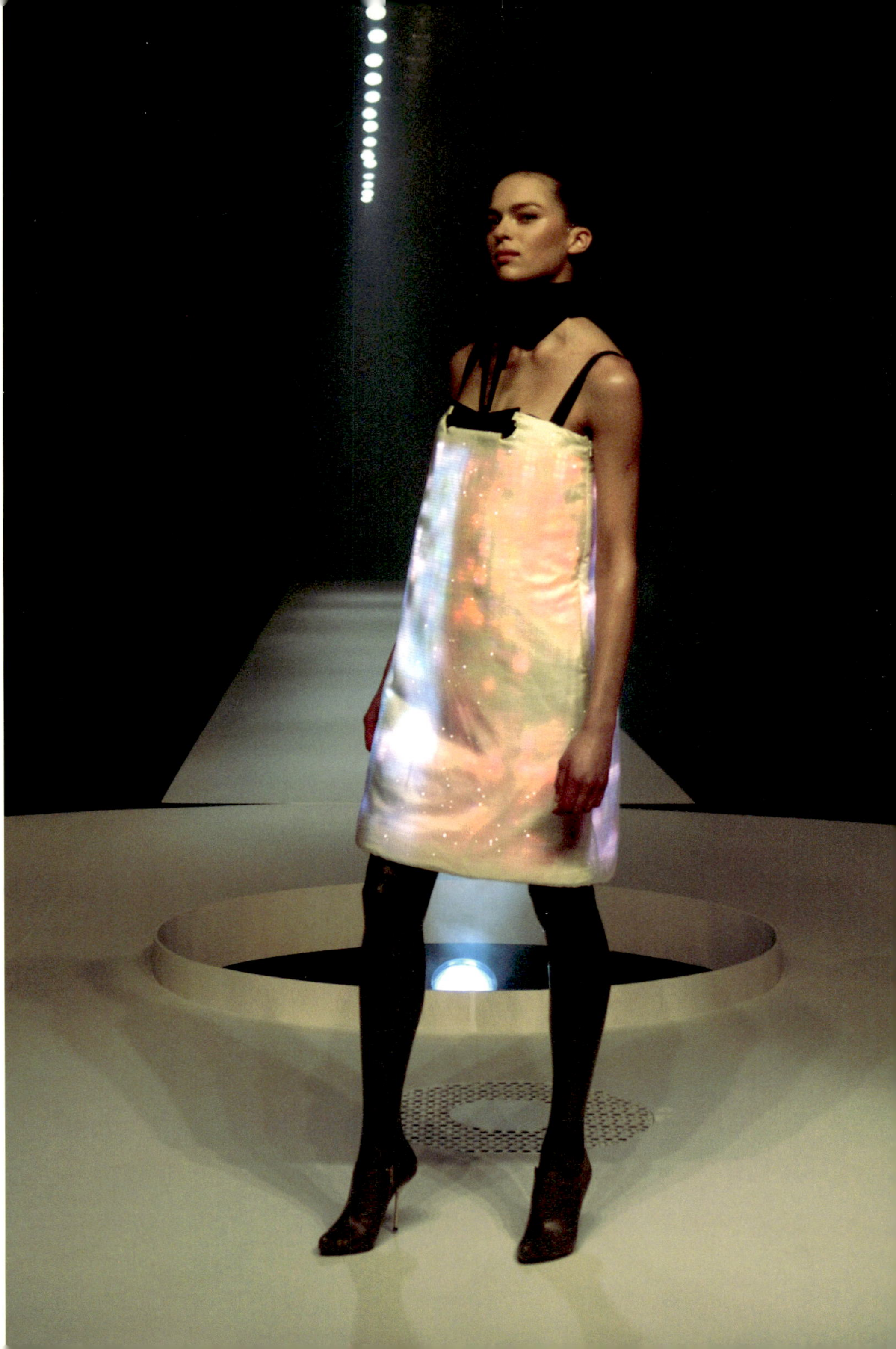

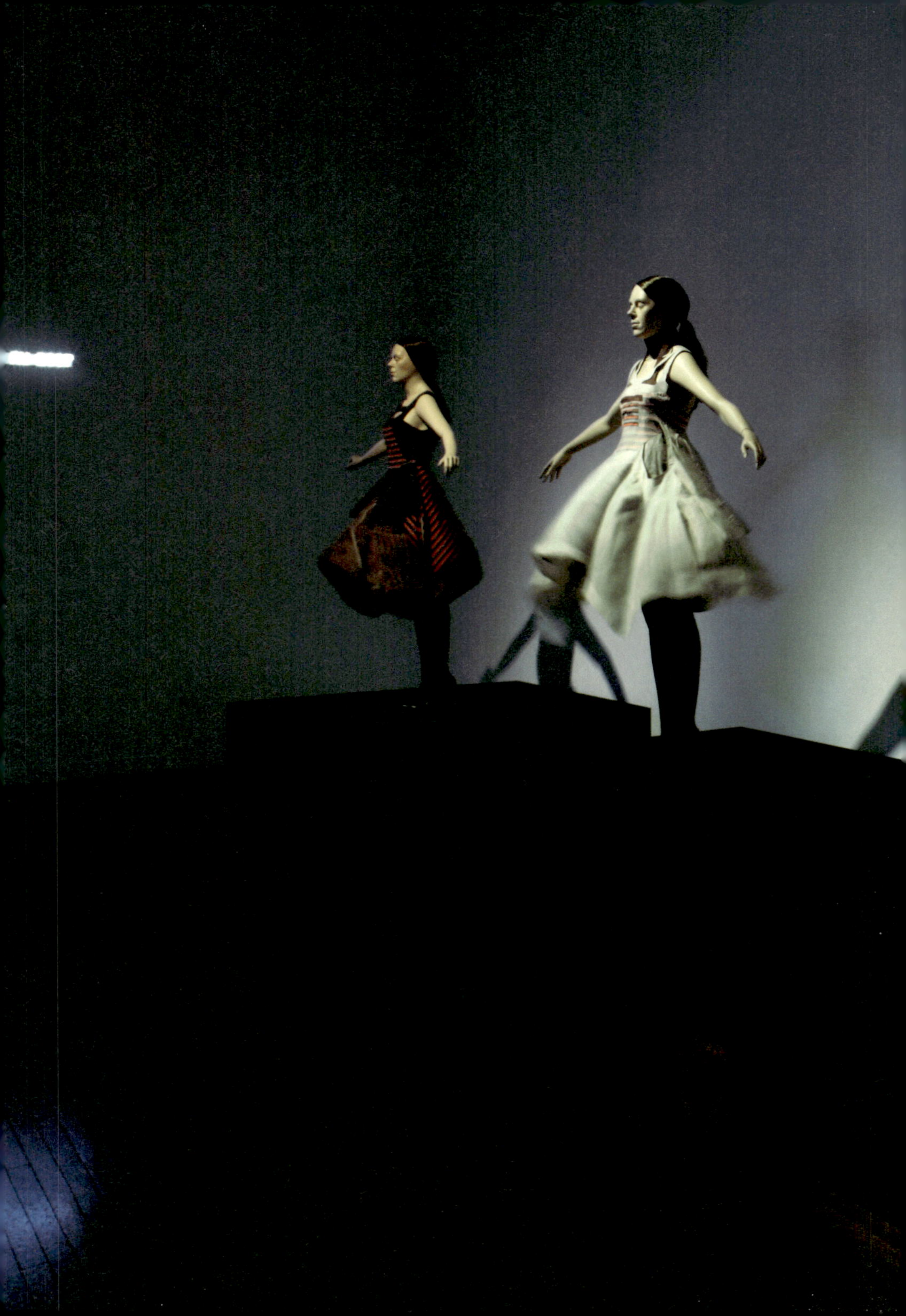

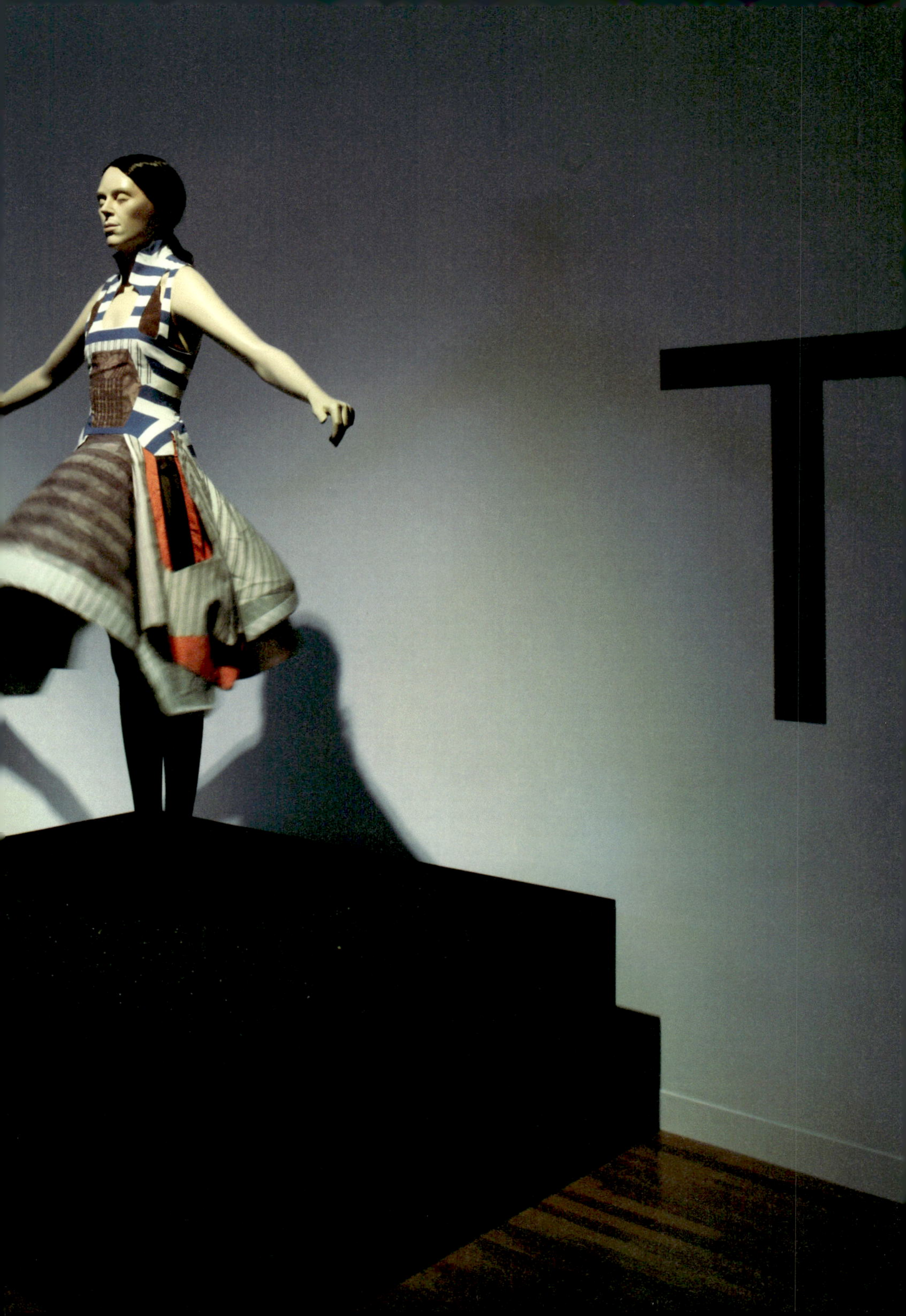

《地からは離れられない》| EARTHBOUND (Autumn/Winter 2009)

《地からは離れられない》を見れば、フセイン・チャラヤンが人間のフォルムにいまなお魅了されていることがわかる。このコレクションは、常に変化する環境に人体がどのように対応していくか、また、絶えず移り変わる中でも変わらずにいたいという願い、あるいは、身の回りの建築物が織りなす景観の発展が身体の形成に投影されていく様に発想を得ている。建築、構造、建設過程、素材などはすべて、このコンセプトを衣服へ置き替える際に不可欠な要素である。本コレクションでは、特別に開発されたボンディング加工の灰色のパファ(ダウンジャケット)が、いわばコンクリートの基礎を想起させる。また、目の細かい黒、白、灰色を織り込んだ彫刻のような生地を、有機的なドレープを描くミニドレスに仕立て、流れるような液状のコンクリートを表現した。灰色のアスファルトの歩道の写真によるプリントは、基礎から地面へとコンセプトを移動させ、ソフトレザーのパンツや、メタルビーズで刺繍を施したプリント柄のシフォンに、質感を与えている。強力なストレッチ素材で作られたコンクリートプリントのビスティエドレスは、ショート丈でタイトなシルエット。これに、ビンテージ加工の大きなサイズのバイカージャケットを組み合わせた。そしてショーの終盤には、建築現場の足場と石をプリントした、ターコイズとコーラルで潤色した服が登場。これらは最後に、鮮やかな色の成形レザー製のバストとヒップが張り付けられた、コンクリート・プリントの柔らかなレザードレスのセクションへと移り変わる。こうした要素を束ねて建築のイメージを作り出し、現実とファンタジーの境目をあいまいにしている。

fig. U

Earthbound affirms Hussein Chalayan's continued fascination with the human form. The collection was inspired by a response to ever changing environments, the desire to stay rooted amidst a constant state of flux and the way in which the development of our architectural landscape can be indicative of the body's gradual formation.

Architecture, structures, building processes and materials all play an integral role in the translation from concept into clothing. The collection evokes concrete foundations through specially developed bonded grey puffa material, whilst sculptural fabric in fine black, white and grey weave is worked into organically draped mini-dresses which suggest concrete in its flowing liquid state. A photographic print of grey asphalt pavement moves the concept from foundations to ground level and adds texture to soft leather trousers and printed chiffon embroidered with metal beading. A concrete print bustier dress in power stretch fabric is cut short and tight and worn underneath an oversized distressed biker jacket. Finally, bright turquoise and coral embellished prints of scaffolding and stone move into a section of specially created vibrantly coloured moulded leather busts and bottoms attached to soft concrete print leather dresses. These elements are incorporated to create the impression of architecture, blurring the gap between reality and fantasy.

《無為な日々を過ごす甘美さ》
DOLCE FAR NIENTE (Spring/Summer 2010)

《無為な日々を過ごす甘美さ》は、6つの異なるグループにデザインされ、ショーはフセイン・チャラヤン自身の司会により進められた。このコレクションは、50年代のシルエットにモンゴルのテイストを加えたスタイルから始まり、90年代風のブラックレザーと白いデニムにストライプがプリントされたジャージー素材を組み合わせたスタイルへと移り変わる。ネイビーブルーのストライプとミルクのようなドレープが登場する場面では、気ままに遊び楽しんでいるような気分と、フランスの保養地ドーヴィルの海を思い起こさせる。最後のグループでは、よじ登ろうとする手のイメージが多用されており、これは現代の上昇志向と野心を表現したものである。

Dolce Far Niente was designed in six distinct groups. The collection moved from 50s inspired silhouettes with a Mongolian influence, through to 90s inspired black leather and white denim worn with printed stripe on jersey. The emergence of navy blue stripes and milk-like draping evoked Dolce Far Niente – the sweetness of doing nothing - and images of the sea at Deauville. The final group was dominated by images of climbing hands, which represent ideas of ascension and aspiration in the present day. Hussein Chalayan was the compère during the show's presentation.

fig. V

《ミラージュ》 | MIRAGE (Autumn/Winter 2010)

チャラヤンの最新コレクション《ミラージュ》は、彼が継続して取り組んできた"旅"という概念を、文字通りの意味だけでなく、比喩的、物理的、あるいは観念的に伝えるものである。このコレクションは、アメリカのロードトリップをモチーフに、旅とともに、ある女性のワードローブの中がどのように変化してきたか、その変遷を見せている。街から海へ抜け、山々を越え、砂漠を横断するというような、様々な州や地域をまたぐ一本道の自動車の旅の進展に合わせて、コレクションは展開されていく。旅の起点はニューヨーク。ウールメランジ製の拡大ヘリンボーン柄の長い丈のコートには、グレーのデニムと、同じ色調のグレーのスニーカーが合わせられ、ワークウェアとストリートスタイルとの衝突が示唆されている。また、後に登場する、チャコールグレーと黒のストライプヘリンボーン地のテーラードジャケットとパリっとした白シャツのコーディネートは、ペンシルバニア州のアーミッシュ・コミュニティに着想しており、クリーンかつシンプルなシルエットを創出している。また、幾重にも重ねられた装飾的なレースやシフォンの間から見えるサッシュ(帯)には、テキサスの歴史劇コンテストの要素が盛り込まれている。スワロフスキーとのコラボレーションにより、結晶化されたメッシュには、暗闇を照らす車のヘッドライトのイメージがプリントされ、夜のドライブという体験が表現されている。舞台がメキシコとの国境付近に移ると、鮮やかな赤やライラック色、黄色のウールニットがラッフルを形作り、あるいは、複雑なかぎ針編みのニットが、レザージャケットの袖やオーバーサイズのカーディガンの身頃といった部分に用いられている。ハリウッドに到着すると、クラシックなテーラードスタイルにフェミニンなスワロフスキーのクリスタルが融合したルックが登場。ここでは、シフォンやシルク、そしてウール地に、ヘリンボーン風ストライプ柄を転写するため、クリスタルの熱転写技術が採用されている。

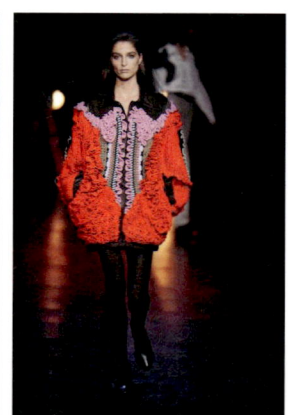

fig. W

Hussein Chalayan's newest collection conveys the idea of the 'journey' - literal, metaphorical, physical and transcendental - a continuing point of reference in Chalayan's work. The collection evolved from the concept of an American road trip and how a journey can shape a woman's wardrobe. Travelling a route that motors across a diversity of states and terrains, from city to sea, through mountains and across desert - a collection is developed as the journey unfolds. The journey begins in New York. A full-length city overcoat in an enlarged Herringbone wool melange is worn with grey denim and tonal grey sneakers, suggesting a collision between work wear and street style. The collection then looks to the Amish community in Pennsylvania for inspiration, with charcoal and black striped herringbone tailored jackets worn over crisp white shirting to create a clean and simple silhouette. Elements evoking Texan Pageant competitions are visible in sashes twisted and trapped between layers of encrusted lace and chiffon. In collaboration with Swarovski, crystallised mesh is printed with the image of car headlights at night, embodying the experience of night-time driving. Inspired by the proximity to the Mexican border, bright wools in red, lilac and yellow are knitted to form ruffles, or intricately crocheted into sections that become the sleeve of a leather jacket or the body of an oversized cardigan. Arriving in Hollywood, a heat transfer crystal technique is used to apply a herringbone-effect stripe to chiffon, silk and wool, combining classic tailoring styles with the femininity of Swarovski crystal.

フセイン・チャラヤンとの対話
聞き手：長谷川祐子

アイデアが生まれる場所

長谷川祐子(YH)：まず最初に、ファッション・デザイナーになろうと思ったきっかけを教えて下さい。

フセイン・チャラヤン(HC)：確かに私はファッション・デザイナーですが、どちらかというと、ファッション・アーティストに近いと思います。自身の仕事のスタンスを考えると、そう形容した方が相応しい気がします。私は、自分のアイデアを身体を通して表現していますし、身体というものにとても興味を持っています。身体というのは、私たちのあらゆる行為の中心に位置するものです。すべては身体を外在化したものではないかと考えています。どんなものでも、結局身体に帰着するのです。アイデアを身体というフィルターを通して見ると、とても生き生きしはじめると感じます。また、身体はこういったアイデアを発展させ、人生をよりよいものにしてくれる。私はいつも、様々なアイデアから構成される服が好きなのです。服で"小さな人生"を創出しようとしているのです。そして、着ること、動くことで、その"人生"はさらに進化すると考えます。それってとても、エキサイティングでしょう？つまり身体は、アイデアにさらなる生命を与えてくれると言うこともできるでしょう。

YH：どのように、そういったアイデアを得るのですか？あなたは12歳までキプロスで過ごしたんですよね。その後、お父さんとロンドンに移られた。あなたのアイデア形成に影響を与えた教育や経験とは、どのようなものですか？

HC：子どもの頃に、異文化の間を行き来したという事実、また、11歳のときに突然、義理の兄妹と一緒に暮らさなければいけなくなったという経験です。見知らぬ人たちがいきなり家にやってきたのです。とても若いときに、このような未知のシチュエーションにさらされたわけです。これは幼い子どもにとっては異常な状況でした。こうした経験が、自分をオープンかつ好奇心旺盛にしたのではないかと思います。私の最大の原動力は、好奇心です。本当に、様々なことに興味があるんです。小さな島の出身だからこそ、そこから世界を発見するというのは、好奇心を一層掻き立てます。なぜなら、ある意味、孤立しているからです。これはもしかすると、600年の鎖国を経た日本の人たちが、開国後、他の国々の文化に熱狂したのと似ているかもしれません。それを個人に置き換えて考えれば、理解しやすいのではないかと思います。好奇心という感覚が増幅するのです。私はまた、子どもの頃に何度も引っ越しをし、学校を転々としました。そういった経験、小さな島の出身であること、あるいは極端に混合培養された場所で育ったということが、私の考え方に影響しているのは確かです。

YH：東西の邂逅、あなたには両方の側面がありますね。

HC：私たちは民族的に、東洋人ではなくて西洋人です。ただし、言語や宗教を通して、私たちは東洋の影響を受けています。私たちは信仰深くはないけれど、文化的な影響は受けています。加えて、私の好奇心の大部分を占めているものは、人々の移動に関してです。人はどのように、ある場所から別の場所へと移動するのかを知りたいという欲求です。オスマン帝国時代、多くのキプロス人は、他の文化圏の人たちと結婚しました。というこ

とはつまり、既に我々はミックスされているというわけです。ある意味私は、そういった事実を分析しようと試みているのです。つまり、好奇心というのはある部分で、脱構築しようという試みでもあります。私は、既に混合培養された文化を持ち、誰がどこの出身か既に見分けがつかなくなった場所から、もう一つの島、イギリスへ移住しました。イギリスでは、多様な人種の共同体が存在しています。例えば日本人コミュニティや中国人コミュニティ、そしてトルコ人やギリシャ人のコミュニティなど。つまり私は、既に様々な要素が混ざり合った文化を持つ場所から、複数の文化が融合した別の島へと移動したのです。こうした経験が、私の知りたいという好奇心を育んだと言えます。私はまた、人間の行動や、文化的コードにも興味があります。コードがどのように人々の行動やそのふるまい方に影響を与えているのか。私はまた、ある場所からやってきて、また別の場所で生活する人々から見出される新たな人類学にも興味があります。彼らがまた別の場所出身の人と結婚すると、そこにまた新たな人類学が生まれるのです。私もある意味その一人だと思います。なぜなら、私はかつてイギリスの植民地だったキプロス出身で、現在はイギリスに住んでいる。でも、私といっしょに働くメンバーは色々な国からやってきています。私は今、ロンドン人なんだと感じています。東京出身だけれど、日本人じゃないという感じ。そう、ロンドンは、ほとんど一つの国と言ってもいいでしょう。これは新たな研究課題であり、私を魅了しています。おそらく、私は身体やファッションを、ある種、科学の一分野として見ているのです。そう、科学のように。

ストーリー・テラー

YH：その「科学」とはどのような意味ですか？
HC：科学と言っても、物理や化学のことを言っているのではありません。研究という名の科学、という意味です。私は物語を通して物事を捉える思考を持っているのかもしれません。ある種のストーリー・テラーですよね。服やショーを通してその物語を語っているのです。また、私は服そのものが大好きなのです、たとえそれが意味を持っていないとしてもね。あるいは、あるコンテクストから派生した服である、という事実が好きです。たとえそれが、自分とは関わり合えないものであったとしても、別に構わない。私が行っていることは物事に対して疑問を投げかけることであり、また、こういった見方もできるよ、と提示することでもあります。世の中にはわからないことが数多くあって、それらを作品制作を通して理解しようとしているのです。自分の作品がそれ自身生命を持ってくれたらと願っています。もっと知りたいという欲求、より深く知るということが、実のところ、私の物語なのです。ただし、私の作品はファンタジーと現実の狭間に位置するものだと考えています。ありふれた日常を自分にとってより面白いものにしようと常に試みていて、それを他の人々と共有したいのです。つまり私の中には、人生に辟易した自分と、人生にワクワクしている自分とが共存しているのです。その意味で私の行っていることは、その2つの間のバランスをとるということだといます。

YH：あなたはよく、物語性について話していますし、最近のコレクションやビデオ作品には、豊かな物語性が内包されています。あなたは文学や既存のストーリーに興味がありますか？ それらを作品の着想源とすることは？
HC：通常そういうことはありません。もちろん読書はしますが、作品は様々な事柄から生まれてきます。ある事柄が別のことに派生する。すべては繋がっているのです。私が抱く興味には、共通点があります。テクノロジーや人類学、物語、空間あるいは空間の意味、国家の意味、文化が持つ意味、地理が文化にどのように影響を与えてきたか、などです。それらを考えるのは、私の出自に関係しています。私は、とても複雑な場所の出身ですから。国家の意味は、伝承されるものです。人種的に意味するものと、政治的に意味するものが、必ずしも一致するとは限りません。私はナショナリズムに覆い隠され、目に見えなくなってしまっている事柄に興味があります。つまり、どのように社会、性、政治における主流の思考が現実を覆い隠してしまっているかということです。ある意味私は、そういった覆いを取り除こうと試みているのです。何層にもかけて覆っているレイヤーがあり、私はそこから埋もれた現実を掘り起こそうとしているのです。ロンドンは私にとってそうした掘り起こすという行為に適した環境です。その一方で、文化的あるいは歴史的な偏見にも興味があります。さらにテクノロジーといったものに対しては、私がただ単純に好きだからです。

なぜ作るのか

YH：あなたのテクノロジーの用い方は、素晴らしいですね。
HC：そうですね。というのも、すべては繋がっているわけですから。私が抱く興味の対象には、明確な理由があったりしますが、なぜ自分がそんなにテクノロジーに興味があるのかはよくわかりません。とにかく、本当に好きなんです。けれど、概して私の知りたいという好奇心は、作品をつくる理由に直結しています。そして作品を通して多くの人に出会い、そういった人との関係性もまた、作品の一部になるのです。つまり作品をつくるということは教育にも似た行為とも言えるでしょう。作品はある意味私を教育し、その過程で他の人々もインスピレーションを得るのではないかと思います。つまり、ある種の宇宙のような、奇妙な小さなハブ（結節点）を作り出しているのです。
YH：レイヤーを剥がすという話は、とても面白い。つまり制作の過程というのは、物語を編むような行為ですね。
HC：そうですね。私がそうする理由は、とても複雑です。要するに、女性のおかげだと言わざるを得ないでしょう。それが、もう一つの大きな理由です。私は男性ではなく、女性に育てられたのです。父親とロンドンに移りましたが、その後すぐ、寄宿学校に行きました。ですから、ほんの短期間しか父親とは暮らしていません。12歳まで、そして16歳から18歳までを、女性に囲まれて生活してきたのです。
YH：母親ですよね？ あなたは一人っ子だと聞いています。
HC：そうです。生い立ちに起因しているのですが、女性を力づけるというのは、私にとって大

きな意味を持っています。実際私の家族では、女性たちは皆、とても強く、個性的でしたが、女性がどんな風に男性に扱われてきたか、私は見てきたのです。
YH：女性は男性に比べて劣った存在であるとか、差別があったということ？
HC：そんなところです。日本でもそうでしょう。つまり、女性は強いけれども、男性は女性を見下すようなところがあったんです。セックスマシーンとか、子を産む機械であるとか、そんなふうに。今はちがいますが、成長の過程でそういったことに影響を受けたのです。また、分断された島の出身であるという事実、つまり、30年もの間、反対側に行くことが許されていなかったという事実は、私に影響を与えました。たとえば、「敵」とは誰なのかと考えるようになりました。同じ人間ではあっても、当時、向こう側にいる人間は敵と見なされていました。これもまた、子どもの頃、私の好奇心を掻き立てるものでした。子ども時代、私はよくギリシャ側から流れてくる川のそばで遊びました。ギリシャ側にある病院から、色々なものが流れてくるのです。そこである日、私は写真を撮ろうとギリシャ側に渡ったんです。あと少しで逮捕されるところでした。まるで映画みたいでしょう。

地中に埋めたドレス

YH：そういった興味が、また新しい物語をつくり出すのですから、とても面白いですね。今でも、あなたの第一作目は伝説的に語られています。一旦地中に埋め、取り出された服のこと。これはある種、発掘ですね。
HC：これは卒業制作《逸脱する流れ》(p.18)の作品です。1992年に制作し始めて、'93年に卒業しました。これは実は、様々な出来事を小さな物語に仕立てたものなのです。要は、デカルト的世界観について言及したものです。そしてこの物語をアクションとしてつくり直しました。具体的には、物語を書き、その物語を実際に演じてみたのです。物語の中で、磁気を持つ服を着たダンサーが登場するのですが、彼女たちが亡くなって、着衣したまま土に埋められるという場面があります。それを再現したのです。
YH：どれくらいの間、洋服を埋めたのですか？
HC：数ヶ月です。いや、最初のものは6ヶ月くらいだったと思います。でもそもそものアイデアは、この状況を再現することでした。これが私の制作方法の始まりです。服がある出来事から派生する過程であり、出来事の結果でもあり、また、服そのものが出来事になるのです。これが原点です。
YH：とても芸術的ですね。処女作からそんなステートメントがあったんですね。これが自分の考え方であり、これが方法論だという。たいへん明快ですね。
HC：とても刺激的な時期で、後にこれを新しい紙と組み合わせました。地中に埋められた服を、当時よく用いていたペーパー・ファブリックとともに発表したんです。そこには文章が書かれていて、まっさらな紙と、埋められて土が付いた服とを一緒に見せたんです。すごく美しいものでした。そしてこれが、次の《エアメール・ドレス》(p.22)に繋がります。多くの重要なプロジェクトが、ここから始まったんです。

YH：これが《エアメール・ドレス》へと繋がるのですか？
HC：つまり、紙のアイデアが繋がったということです。紙のアイデアをさらに発展させたのです。何かが地球に還るとか、空に向かうというアイデアがとても気に入ったのです。しかし、これは後に展開するプロジェクトで、卒業制作とはちがいます。卒業制作では、磁気によって異質な素材が相互に作用する服をつくろうと試みました。これは、プロジェクトに付随する小さな物語の中でも言及されます。物語の中で描かれるダンス・パフォーマンスの場面で、パフォーマンス中に鉄くずがダンサーに向かって投げ付けられます（彼らは服が磁気を持っていることを知っていて、ダンサーたちを困らせようとしたのです）。ダンサーらはパフォーマンス終了後、誘拐され、殺され、埋められてしまうのです。むちゃくちゃな話に聞こえますが、鉄くずと磁気の物語は、ここから来たのです。このように、プロジェクトは始まりました。
YH：こんな大きな反響があったことに、驚かれたでしょう。あなたはまだ、とても若かったですし。
HC：23歳でした。とても驚きました。求職中でしたし、自分のブランドを始めることすら想像していませんでした。

歴史の始まり

YH：この作品の後、あなたは数多くの興味深い作品を生み出しました。例えばあなたがさきほど触れた《エアメール・ドレス》。この作品は、紙から着想したとか。そういう連続性がとても面白いですね。本作とあなたの初期作品には、何か共通点がありますか？
HC：《エアメール・ドレス》は最初のコレクションから始まりました。ここから、様々な方法を試みました。このジャケットはビョークにあげたものですが、彼女はアルバム『ポスト』のカバーで着ています。現在はメトロポリタン美術館かNYのどこかの美術館が所有していると思います。
YH：再生産はしなかったのですか？
HC：していません。当時作ったものだけです。このアイデアをさらに進めて、エアメール・クロージングをシリーズとして発表しました。もう一度やってみたいですね。この後に、Tシャツも作りました。パッケージからはぎ取ると、その断片がTシャツに残る仕組みです。すごくエキサイティングでした。本当に、もう一度取り組んでみたいと思っています。Tシャツは布製ですが、部分的に紙がくっついていて、Tシャツはパッケージに貼付けられているんです。パッケージを取ると、その小片が残るのです。コンセプトは、郵便で送ることのできる服というものです。さらに進化させて、ニットウェアでもやってみたかったのですが、お金がかかるし、投資も必要ですから。私たちは封筒に様々な言語を記しました。これにより、どこにでも送ることができるし、誰でもこれを読んでコンセプトを理解することができます。ぜひとも復活させたいですね。
YH：実際どんなものなのかイメージはありますか？

HC:《束の間の瞑想》(p.30)という映像作品の中に登場しています。作品の冒頭で、Tシャツがパッケージである封筒に梱包されるシーンがあります。
YH:アイデアが連続していくということ、そしてそのアイデアの発展のさせ方は、とても美しい流れを描いていると思います。流れているようだもの。
HC:パッケージングというアイデアに取り付かれているんです。パッケージが大好きだし、それを剥ぎ取るとか、破るという行為も好きです。「冷たさ」や「温かさ」を持つ服に惹かれます。私自身、冷たく、温かい人間なのでしょう。
YH:「冷たさ」と「温かさ」という言葉を抽象的につかっていますね。
HC:つまり、服はあるアイデアから生まれてくるが、その時点では「温かい」。一方で、一旦パッケージされてしまうと、冷たく、人間味のないものになる。そのコントラストが好きなんです。パッケージされると、たちまち制度的になるでしょう。そういった制度的なるものが、とても気になるんです。制度とは、行動や秩序を規定するもの。セントラル・セント・マーティンズ在学中から、そういった制度にとても興味を抱いていました。
YH:あなたの作品は、建築的であるとも言われます。これもまた、ある概念に関連することですか?
HC:そう思います。ただ、私が興味があるのは、単なる建物ではなく、建築理論です。それが持つ意味により惹かれるんです。そのことをよく物語っているプロジェクトが、《場所でない場所》(2003年秋冬)です。これはメンズウェアのプロジェクトで、このコレクションの服の購入者は、服のラベルに記されている特定の日時に、ロンドンのヒースロー空港に来るよう招かれます。そこで、その服を着ている人たちに、ポケットの中に入っているものにまつわる話を語り合ってもらおうと考えました。着ることで、服は意味を獲得し、その服が持つ思

い出が多ければ多いほど、その人生はより豊かになるのです。つまり服が、ある出来事を生み出すきっかけとなるわけです。この服を買った誰もが、その場所に行くことができます。しかも、実際にやってきた人がいたんです。ものすごく感動しました。その服が完成するまで、約9ヶ月も費やしましたからね。そして、彼は来たんです。しかもその後、私は彼にスーパーマーケットでバッタリ会ったのです。実は、空港で彼に会ったのは私ではなく、私のスタッフだったのですが、スーパーで彼は私のところにやってきて、「フセイン・チャラヤンさんですね」と聞いてきたのです。「そうです」と答えると、「私がその時の……」というふうに。衝撃的でした。

YH：とても美しいですね。

HC：つまりこのアイデアは、服は人と人とが出会うきっかけになるのだということを物語っています。このように、例えば待合室のような非個人的な場所がちょっとしたイベントに変わる瞬間をつくり出す引き金になるということもあります。すなわち、服は"場所"でもあるのです。私はこれを、建築的だと思っています。形式ではなく、空間の概念であり、空間が意味し得るものという点において建築的なのです。人と出会うことによって、その空間を別の場所へと変化させるのです。

身体への執着

YH：「飛行機ドレス」はシールドのようでもありますね。身体を保護するもののようにも見え、とても構造的です。こういった固い素材で女性を包むというアイデアについて、お話頂けますか？

HC：ここでは、身体を再構築するとか、直立状態に保つというコンセプトがあります。特にこのコレクションの中には、私がデザインした外科手術用のコルセットもありました。つまり、身体をまっすぐに維持するという考えです。実はノアの箱船に基づいていて、このコンセプトを天災に繋げて表現しようと考えていました。洪水が発生し、そこに船があるといった場面を想定したのです。このショーでは、モデルたちに水の中を歩かせたかったのですが、実現できませんでした。災害の後という設定だったんです。荒波に襲われ、軽傷を負った人の身体を、私たちはまっすぐに維持させなければならないというストーリーです。他にも似たようなアイデアが用いられた作品があります。私は、外科手術的に再構築するものに興味があります。

YH：コルセットについて話す人もたくさんいます。

HC：中には、コルセットを拘束的なものであると捉える人もいます。でも実のところ、いくつか異なる見方ができると思うのです。私にとってコルセットは、拘束というより、身体を再構築するもの。とはいえ、人々がこんな感じで歩いて欲しいとは思っていませんが。アイデアとして、です。

YH：例えば、《エコーフォーム》（1999年秋冬）の中にある「飛行機ドレス」や、飛行機座席の頭部が服の一部になっているものは、身体の再構築というアイデアに基づいているのですか？

HC：第一に、こうした乗り物の多くは身体のような存在であると思います。多くの乗り物のデザインは身体のようであり、超高速の中での身体をイメージしていると思うのです。ここで何がしたかったかというと、身体から派生しているものを考察し、それを再び身体に投影し直すということです。

YH：つまりあなたは、身体そのものについて言及しているということですね。こういった類いのメタファーが、スピードや移動を表現していたとしても、結局は身体の話に帰着するということですか？

HC：そうです。身体から派生しているもの、ある種身体から増幅したものを、再び身体に戻したというわけです。建築や建物、私たちがシステムを構築する方法、乗り物をデザインする方法などはすべて、ある意味、身体に類似しています。私たちは、身体を再現しているとも言えるでしょう。私がやりたかったのは、こうした身体が基となっているものを、再び身体に戻すということです。車の内装でさえ、身体のネガであると言えるわけです。私たちの行為すべてが、身体の増幅なのです。だから、それらに目を向けて、再び身体上に戻すということをやってみたらどうかと考えたのです。これが根本にある考えです。このプロジェクト全体を《エコーフォーム》と名付けました。

YH：いつも独特のネーミングで、あるものは造語のようですが、あなたがすべてを考えているのですか？

HC：一連の過程の中で生まれてきます。ときにはタイトルを友人との会話から思い付くこともありますが、大抵の場合、アイデアが浮かんだら、まずそれを誰かに投げかけてみるのです。そこにテーマがあれば、タイトルは自然と出てきます。

定められたものへのまなざし

YH：《パノラマ》(p.24)の中の本展出品作品と《ビトウィーン》(1998年春夏)のイスラム的装束とは、どのような関係性ですか？ 顔を隠して匿名的にするという意味で非常に象徴的な作品ですね。

HC：実は、《パノラマ》は《ビトウィーン》の後に作ったものです。テーマは異なりますが、信念体系を介して、いかに私たちが自分たちの領域を規定しているのかについて脱構築する試みです。というのも、こうしたことが領域を定義づけているからです。特に集団における信念体系に目を向けた場合、私たちを規定するものが見えてきます。私は、どうしたらそれを分析できるか考えてきました。それがある意味、生にも死にもなり得るという考えも気に入りました。こうやって私たちは生まれ、育てられてこのようになった、といったように、あまりにシンプルであるという事実に、私はとても感心したのです。またある意味、このイスラム的コードを通して、人がどのように個性を奪われていったのか、ということにも。これは実は、私にとって非常に重要なプロジェクトです。現在起こっているイスラム教をめぐる様々な出来事よりずっと以前のプロジェクトなのです。とても早かったと思います。つまりこれは、「領域の定義」であり「育成／自然」であり、さらに「生／死」でもあるのです。《パノラマ》は言語

と言語の制約について考えたコレクションです。なぜ言語か？その理由は、どのように人々は言語を通して物事を定義づけているのかと考えたとき、言語では説明できないものを作ってみたいと思ったからです。ここで登場する服装は、どこかの民族的な衣装であるのか、あるいは、何か奇妙な儀式のための衣装なのか、特定することはできない。私がここで試みたこととは、定義し得ない新しいユニフォームを生み出すことでした。それが、このコレクションのねらいです。ショーで鏡を使用したことで、登場する服は反響し合い、また反射した。自らが作り出したパラメーターの中で、身体が失われていく。ですから言語の制約や、文化や信念体系の制約、これらは人間によって作られるものですが、その中で、自分自身を喪失してしまうという考えが背後にありました。本コレクションは非常に複雑なもので、そのプロセスは私にとって重要なものですが、他の人々はそのプロセスから生まれてくるものしか関心を示しません。アーティストやデザイナーにとってはこうしたプロセスはとても重要です。一方で、一般の人々にとって、結果こそが大切なのであり、プロセスを知る必要はないのです。

YH：あなたのショップにとても興味があります。実際に着ることができる洋服を売る場所でありながら、コレクションの背景にあるコンセプトを見せる場所でもあるのでしょうか？

HC：そこを訪れた人が背後にあるコンセプトを知る必要は必ずしもありません。正直、服を気に入ってもらって、それを美しいと思ってもらえたら、それで十分なんです。ショップではコレクションの一部を販売していますが、どちらかと言うとプレゼンテーションの場として考えています。ただ、服はショーの構成要素になりますし、またショーのきっかけにもなることがあります。

YH：ショップでは、パフォーマンスのビデオを流したりはしないのですか？

HC：もちろんします。そういった場所があれば。でも、ご存知のように、ここには困難な問題がありました。私は自分のショップを本当に必要としています。ショップではなく、自分の空間が欲しい。ものを売る場所であるからといって、ショップと呼ぶのは好きではありません。むしろ、空間であって欲しい。東京で以前、期間限定のショップをやったとき、2階でビデオを上映したんです。一時的なプロジェクトではありましたが、すごく頑張ってつくりました。たくさんのことを、この経験から学んだんです。

YH：以前に代官山のショップをオープンされたときは、ビデオの展示も含め、オリーブの鉢を配るなど、大変印象的なオープニングでした。あなたの作品がどのような過程を経てできてくるのか、教えてください。

HC：人生というのは、いかに物事をシンプルにしていくかです。物事を単純化するという行為は、実は最も難しいことだと思います。何かを付け足していく方が簡単なんです。まず、アイデアがないといけないけれど、次にそれをいかに整理していくか、その方法も知っている必要があります。それにはスキルが必要です。デザイナーの多くは、たくさんの要素を加えていくけれども、どうすれば取り除けるかを知らないんです。とても難しいことなんですけどね。

チームワーク

YH：あなたの服は、あなたがすべてのデザインを実際に担っているのですか？
HC：ほとんどのものは私がデザインしますが、やはりすべては無理なので、手伝ってもらいます。たとえば、技術的なことは私にはできません。だから、チームで仕事をしています。
YH：チームとの共同作業や、外部の専門家とはどのように作業するのですか？あなたの作品は新しいアイデアやフォームに満ちています。それをどのように、他者と共有するのか、とても興味深いです。
HC：立体裁断を行うスタッフがいますし、パターンを引く者もいます。なので、彼らのもとへアイデアを持っていき、彼らが立体裁断の作業に取りかかる、という具合です。そこに私が修正を加えて、彼らが再び作り直す……その繰り返しです。それがプロセスの一つで、生地のプリントにおいても、同じです。私のアイデアに基づいて、彼らが作るという感じです。それからデザインチーム、あるいは製造の専門家が布地の制作に加わることができればそうするし、細部について話し合ったりするのです。またスタジオには、シニア・デザイナーのようなスタッフがいます。この人が私を様々な面でサポートするのです。布地やバリエーションの計画を手助けしたり、私がアトリエを不在にするときは、他のデザイナーたちの面倒を見ます。でも大半のコレクションは、私が線を引いて、発展させます。ドローイングのときもありますし、あるときは布地を先に決めて、これをこういう風にしたいと伝えたり、細部から進化させるということもあります。つまりはプロジェクトによりけりなのです。なので、もちろん私には手伝ってくれる人々が必要ですし、自分だけではできません。不可能ですから。
YH：《111》(p.56)のような可動式のドレスを作った際、リサーチをしたのですか？
HC：もちろんです。大人数のチームで取り組みました。中には電気系統のエンジニアに、プログラマーに、メカニカルなエンジニアなどがいました。
YH：でも彼らはドレスを作った経験はなかったでしょう？どのように、彼らと仕事を進めたのですか？
HC：これは実験だったんです。だから費用もとても高くついたし、時間もかかりました。
YH：あなたのチームや、あなた自身の領域横断的な統制力に多大な興味を持っている人は多いと思います。なぜなら通常は、情報やネットワークはその専門領域内に限定されていることが多いからです。たとえ、ある人がロボット工学の専門家であるとわかっていても、彼らと仕事をするのが本当に効果的かどうかなど、わからないでしょう。あなたがどのように適切な人材を見つけ出しているのか、とても興味があります。
HC：そうですね。重要なことはコミュニケーションをとることです。私はコミュニケーション能力に長けていると自分では思います。それに、きちんと説明さえできれば、彼らは自分がプロジェクトの一部であると感じてくれるはずですし、人を引き込めるはずです。私一人では、メカニカル・ドレスを制作することなんて、到底無理ですから。
YH：領域横断と言葉でいうのは簡単ですが、実現はそんなに簡単なことではないですから

ね。ロボット工学を研究している人たちは、メカニックのことはわかっても、アートやファッションのことはわかりませんよね。
HC：はい。中には、想像力に欠ける人もいますよ。

着られない服が物語るもの

YH：では次に、《ビフォア・マイナス・ナウ》(p.40)について伺いたいと思います。心惹かれるタイトルですが、作品を見るからに、とても抽象的で多くの意味が込められているようです。このタイトルが意味するものとは何ですか？
HC：これは抽象的なタイトルで、時間の概念と遊ぶことが目的でした。現在について私たちはどのように語っているのか。このプロジェクトはまた、様々な力や重力、そして不可視なものについて探求したものでした。私がここで関心を持ったのは、重力や磁力、電子力です。それは浸食する力であり、何かを付加する不可視なものであり、または、目には見えないものによってインスパイアされるものとも言えるでしょう。どうしたらある形を生み出す手段として、自然の力を用いることができるだろうかと考えました。そこで思い付いたのが、「ビフォア・マイナス」という言葉です。「ナウ」というのは、何もないところから形を獲得するという概念です。つまり、ここには何もなかったけれど、何かが生まれたということ。何かを取り去ったり、はたまた何かを加えたり。それで、失っているもの、あるいは目に見えないもの、だからこそそこから何かを生み出すことができる、そういった概念と遊ぶことはとてもいい方法だと思ったんです。それゆえ、とても抽象的なタイトルになったのです。
YH：なるほど。あなたのコンセプトは、洗練されている一方で、時に難解でもあります。コレクションや映像、美術館での展覧会などのプレゼンテーションを通してそれらは理解されていきます。コンセプトに関してですが、《111》で提起されている111年という期間の長さにはどのような意味があるのでしょうか。
HC：移動という概念はすべてここから始まっています。《111》では、とりわけ服の時代を変えるということに焦点を当てています。なので、このアイデアは非常に進化したので、次のステップとしては、これを完全に着ることのできる服に仕上げることです。服を買って、それを変形することができる、という……本当に壮大な夢ですね。日本企業の支援が得られれば素晴らしいですけど。普段、普通に着ているジャケットが、食事に出かけるためにイブニング・ジャケットに変化する。同じジャケットだけれど、何かしら形を変えることができるようにデザインされている。実現したら、本当にエキサイティングですよね。でも、もしやるならば、洗濯ができるものである必要がありますが。
YH：ではこのコレクションにおいて、着用可能な服として提案されているのはどんなものですか？ あなたのコレクションは、プレゼンテーション用のモニュメント的なドレスと、実用的な服が一緒に提示されることがありますよね。
HC：そうですね。モニュメント的な服が着用可能なドレスへと繋がっていく、と考えています。モニュメント的な作品とそこから派生する作品とが隣り合わせになっているその二重

性が好きなのです。着ることで、モニュメント的な作品の寿命を延ばすことができるというのは、ある意味、とてもモダンだと思います。あるコレクションのドレスをあなたにプレゼントしたとしても、よりモニュメント的なドレスの中に、その片鱗を見ることができるのです。

YH：あなたの方法論や考え方はファッション関係者にとって大変啓発的ですよね。コレクションのショーとコンセプトテキスト。ショップで、着用可能な商品とともに、例えばビデオなどでショーのドキュメントや映像作品を見せることができたら、理想的ですね。

HC：もちろん。私が試みていることは、身体と服を用いてマイクロ地理学を作ることです。そしてまた、プロセスの頂点に達したものとしてモニュメント的な作品を見せることが、プロジェクトの究極の段階です。そして、あらゆるものがそこにうまく調和している状態が、私が目指すところです。仮にプロジェクトのピークを何らかの形で見せるとしたら、プロジェクトの全体像を見せるでしょう。素敵なトップスやシャツを一枚見せるよりもね。その一方で、その服の良さだけで、人が手に取ってくれて、着てくれたら、それはもちろん素晴らしいことだと思います。ただ欲を言えば、もし自分のショップやコーナーがあれば、プロセスをもっと見せたいし、少なくともモニュメント的な作品だけでも見せたいですね。

YH：例えば、《アフター・ワーズ》(p.28)コレクション。パフォーマンスとしても、有名な作品です。一つの例として、モニュメンタルな作品と実用的な服の関係を説明してください。

HC：そうですね、両者は関係しています。これは、ある東欧人のワードローブに見立てたコレクションです。コートとドレスが登場するが、2つは関係し合っていて、デザインもよく似ていて、色のコントラストも似通っているが、このショーには他のセクションもあるのです。仮に一つのセクションだけを見たとしたら、単なるドレスにしか見えず、これがいったい最後にどのように繋がっていくのかわからないかもしれない。しかし、コレクション全体を見てみると、ショーには異なる章がいくつもあることがわかるでしょう。そして最後に、登場人物は家を出ようとしていて、ガーメント・カバーも持っていこうとしていることがわかる。なぜなら、これは戦時中、襲撃の最中に、まさに所有物を隠そうとしている場面だからである。一部だけを見ると何の関連性もないように見えるから、全体を見る必要があるのです。だからこそのコレクションなのです。

《アフター・ワーズ》のコレクションを通して見ると、これは、誰かのワードローブのようであり、例えば花柄の生地の様式から、東欧出身の人のワードローブだとわかる。モデルによって服へと変化する椅子カバーの裏地にも、このパターンは用いられています。このプロジェクトはコソボ紛争がきっかけとなり、よく似た状況を経験したキプロスの紛争に関連づけたのです。キプロスをギリシャに併合しようとする計画の中で、ギリシャのEOKA（キプロス闘争民族組織）の支持者たちがトルコ系キプロス人の家々を襲撃した際に起こった出来事を基にコレクションを構成したのです。ショーにおける最後のシーンは、残された椅子をトランクに、リビング用のテーブルをスカートに変形させることで、家を追われても、自分の財産を持って逃げることができるというものでした。

YH：あなたのショーは、コンセプトを伝えるための一つのパフォーマンスのようですね。とてもアーティスティックですが、一度きりですから限られた人しか見られない。

コンテクストの中で

HC：私はファッション・デザイナーですから、このように見せることしかできません。コンテクストの中で、服を見せるのです。なぜなら、仮に椅子のカバーだけのコレクションを作ったら、自分自身があまりに縛られるし、そんなコレクションでは、何も売ることさえできないでしょう。売ることのできる服を作ることで、コレクションを支えているのです。だから、様々な方法で複数の要素を関連づける必要があります。同じように展覧会カタログの制作においても、どのように編集するかが非常に大切でしょう？ 私の最新コレクション《ミラージュ》(p.68)でも同じことです。これもまた、アメリカのロードトリップに出かけた架空の人のワードローブに見立てたものです。

YH：では2009年の《地からは離れられない》(p.64)はどうですか？

HC：これは地中に潜って行くというコンセプトで、地中の断面を表現した服が多く登場します。これは一つ前のシーズンの《慣性》(p.20)に対するリアクションでもあり、《慣性》では、スピードの結果としての地球の衝突をテーマにしました。つまり、《地からは離れられない》は、ある場所からここではない別の世界に想像を巡らせるというものとは、対極的なものです。本コレクションの中で、私はまるで岩盤のような、非常に特殊な生地を用いました。同時にここには、性的苦しみもあります。ある種、肉体的にSMのような要素も孕んでいるのです。現実性という概念だけでなく、性的苦しみという概念も気に入りました。肩の部分は、成型皮革でできています。これは私がよく用いる首まわりの造作です。2つの異なる生地を組み合わせています。

YH：デザインする中で、生地のアイデアはあるのですね。あなたの説明を聞いていると、まるで彫刻作品を作っているような感覚ですし、本当に生地に詳しいですね。

HC：はい。とても単純に見える生地でも、実はウールとシルクが一枚になった、特別に開発された生地だったりします。私はこのように、2つの要素が融合した生地が好きです。単なる黒のドレスでも、一枚の布がウールからシルクに変化しているのです。縫い目なしに。直近の3つのコレクションで私が目指したのは、着ることのできる作品をショーで見せることでした。考え抜かれた作品ですが、バイヤーたちには、それでも見かけ倒しのように捉えられてしまいます。ですから、私は最近、着ることのできるものにエネルギーを注いでいるのです。ただ、着るにはよほど自信がないと着られないかもしれません。ですから私の理想としては、自分の環境を手に入れること。できればロンドンに空間を持ちたいですね。単なるショップではなく、服を飾り、それを人が自由に見て、買うこともできるスペースが欲しいです。"ギャラリー兼ショップ"のような。

YH：人々があなたのコンセプトに出会い、体験できるスペースですね。それは美術館のアルターモデルということもできますね。あなたはアートとデザインの両方に刺激を与えながら、どんどん再領域化しているカタリストといえます。同じようなクリエイターが若い世代から出てくることを期待したいと思います。

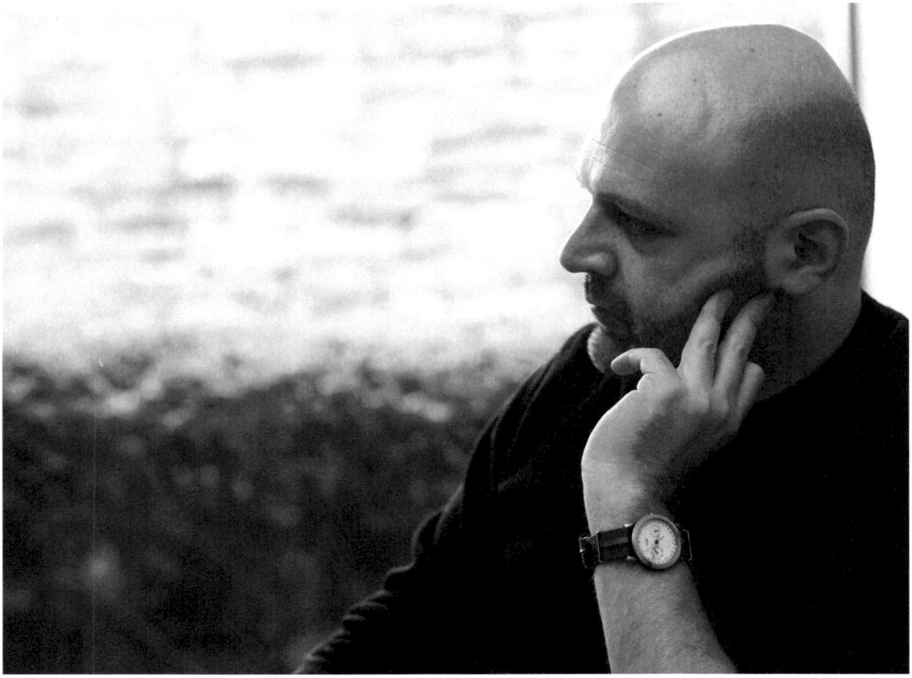

Hussein Chalayan Interview
Interviewer: Yuko Hasegawa

Yuko Hasegawa (YH): First, I want to ask you why did you decide to become a fashion designer after your studies?
Hussein Chalayan (HC): Well I'm a fashion designer but I think I'm more like a fashion artist because of the way I work. I express my ideas through the body, because I am really excited about the body. And I feel like the body is the center of everything we do. Everything is an externalization of the body. Everything really comes down to the body. So, I feel that if ideas are filtered through the body, they become more alive. Also, the body will take those ideas and take the life further. So, I always like clothes which are compositions of my ideas. I try to create a "mini life" with the clothes. And then through use and movement, I think that life goes further. I find that idea really exciting. That in a way the body gives the ideas a further life.
YH: How do you get those ideas. I read about your history, that is your childhood of 12 years in Cyprus. Then you moved to London with your father. So, what kind of education and experiences helped you to form those kinds of ideas?
HC: I think the fact that I've moved between very different cultures, back and forth, from a young age. And my experience when I was eleven to suddenly have to share the house with my step-sister and brother. So, these strangers suddenly came to the house. I think from a young age I was exposed to some alien situations that were very unusual for a young child. And I think it's made me very open and also very curious. My biggest drive is my curiosity. Also because I'm from a small island, to discover the world from a small place makes you more curious, because in a way you feel isolated. Maybe this is a bit like the fact how Japan was closed for 600 years and the Japanese, in a way they went crazy for the rest of the world after opening up. So, if you can imagine a version of that in a personal way, where you've been in an isolated place, so your sense of curiosity increases. I also went back and forth a lot as a child. I changed schools a lot. So, it's a combination of that and also I think coming from an island, we have a very mixed culture, super-mixed.
YH: West meets East and you have both aspects, don't you?
HC: I think that in my case, racially we're not Eastern, racially we're European. But we have the Eastern influence through language and obviously religion. We are not religious, but we have the cultural influence. And I think that also, a lot of my curiosity lies in wanting to know movements of people. How people move from one place to another. And I think because in the Ottoman Empire, there we so many people cross-marrying, that in a way the mixture is already in us. I'm trying to, in a way dissect it, so the curiosity is partly to do with trying to deconstruct it. I've gone from one place which is already a mixture and we can't see any more who's from where and I've gone to another island which is England where you can see the groups of people. Like you can see the Japanese community, the Chinese community, the Turkish, the Greek whatever. So, in a way I've gone from one mixture, which is already blended, to another where I'm seeing it as an island where there's integration as well. This is something that really feeds me, this curiosity of wanting to know. I am also interested in behavior and cultural codes. How the codes affect behavior and manner. I'm also interested in this new anthropology of people that come from one place and they've lived in another place. They marry somebody else from an-

other place, so there's this new anthropology as well. I think I'm one of them, in a way, because I'm from Cyprus. which was a British colony, I now live in England but my team is from everywhere else. I feel like I'm a Londoner now really. So that's like being from Tokyo but not being Japanese. London is almost like a country. This is a new study in itself, that fascinates me. I think I also see the body and fashion as a kind of a world science. I see it like a science.

YH: What exactly do you mean by "science"?

HC: Yes, I do. I don't mean science in like physics and chemistry. I mean science as a study. So, I feel like I have a narrative way of thinking. I'm like a storyteller. And I really say it through the clothes and the shows. I also just really like clothes, just on their own, without having a meaning. Or I like the fact that it's come from a context and even if it's just a particle that you can't associate with, that's fine. I think that in a way, my work is questioning things, but also trying to say you can look at it this way. I'm trying to understand things through the work because there are a lot of things I don't understand. I hope that the work creates its own sense of life. You want to know more about it. So, knowing more is normally my story. But essentially I think that my work is in that gap between fantasy and reality. I'm trying to make ordinary life more interesting for myself and I'm trying to share it with people. So, I guess I lie between really bored with life and being really excited with life. And I think the work is sort of there to create a balance.

YH: You often talk about the narrative. Your recent collections and your video works are full of rich narratives, so are you also interested in literature or existing stories? Do you use these as resources for your works?

HC: Normally, I don't. Of course, I read, but normally, my work comes from things. That is, one thing leads to another. I think everything is connected. And I think that a lot of my interests have things in common, that is technology, anthropology, story, space, meaning of space, meaning of a nation, meaning of culture, how geography has affected culture because I come from a very complicated place. The meaning of nation is handed down. Racially it could be one thing and politically it could be another thing. I'm interested in all these things that are covered up by nationalism. I think what it comes down to, is looking at how social, sexual, political mainstreams cover up reality. And in a way I'm trying to uncover it. There are a lot of layers that are covered up, and in a way I'm trying to dig it out. London has given me the facility to dig it up. I'm interested in cultural and historic prejudice too, that's another side. And things like technology, I'm simply excited by.

YH: It's fantastic how you use technology.

HC: Yes, because they are all connected. There are certain things however, I don't know why I'm interested in them, but I just am. Generally my curiosity of wanting to know is why I do the work. And through the work I meet a lot of people and then the relationships, even that is a part of the work. So, the work is in a way an education as well. Although I start it, it kind of educates me and I think other people get inspired in the process as well, so I think it creates a weird kind of mini hub, like a universe in itself.

YH: It's very interesting your talking about how you're just uncovering layers. And

you know in the process you're kind of knitting a story.
HC: Yes. Also my reasons are quite complex, I think I have to say, because of women. That's another big reason. Because I was raised by women, not men. I moved with my father but then I went to a boarding school. I lived with him very shortly. During my childhood that is until I was 12 and then again from 16 to 18 I was always around women.
YH: Your mother, right? You were an only child?
HC: Yes. Because of my upbringing, for me empowering women is a big thing. Because although actually the women in my family they were all strong, and individualistic, I saw how they were treated by men.
YH: Was there any discrimination? Were women considered to be inferior?
HC: Kind of, like here in Japan, I think it's the same. Women are strong but the men kind of look down on them. You know, they're like sex-machines, and baby-machines, and whatever. It's different now but growing up I was affected by that. Also the fact that I come from a divided island, which means that I couldn't go to the other side for 30 years, this affected me. So the curiosity of wanting to know the "enemy." We're the same people but they're supposed to be "the enemy". This is another thing that fed my curiosity as a child. You know, I would play by the river which came from the Greek side and would find all these objects that had floated down from this hospital on the Greek side. And then one time, I escaped to the Greek side to do a photographic shoot and we nearly got arrested. It was like being in a film.
YH: I think your curiosity is really great. It motivates you to create new narratives. That's very interesting. Still now, people often talk about your first piece. You buried the clothes in the ground and then you dug them up. It's a kind of excavation.
HC: It was for my graduation. I started it in '92 and I graduated in '93. Actually, I created this mini story of events. And it was all about the Cartesian world view. Actually I recreated the story as an action. That idea came from recreating the story. So, basically I created the story, and then I actually performed the story. So, there was a moment in it where these dancers who had magnetic clothes, they died and they were buried with their clothes. So, I recreated that.
YH: How long did you leave the clothes buried?
HC: A few months, or was it 6 months or so, the first one. But the idea was that I recreated this situation again. That's where my way of working started. It is a process where the clothes come from an event, or they're a result of an event, or they're the event themselves. So that's where it started.
YH: It's really very artistic. At the very beginning you just make some statement. This is my way of thinking. This is my kind of methodology. It's quite clear.
HC: It was a really exciting time and I mixed that with this fresh paper. I had the buried clothes and I presented them with this paper fabric I was working with a lot. It had text on it and I showed the crisp white paper and the buried soiled garments together. I thought it was really beautiful. And then from there I started doing The Airmail Clothes. So a lot of important things started from there.
YH: It's connected to *The Airmail Dress* (p.22)
HC: The idea of paper is connected. I took the paper idea further and I liked this

idea of something going to the earth and something going to the sky. This was a later stage. My graduation piece wasn't to do with that. For my graduation piece, I was trying to make clothes that interact with each other magnetically, which was also discussed in a mini narrative which accompanied the project. This narrative depicted a dance performance where iron filings were thrown on the dancers during their performance (knowing that the clothes were magnetic, it was done to confuse them) and the dancers were kidnapped, murdered and buried after their performance. This all sounds out of context but the story of the iron filings and the magnetics came from this. That's how it started.

YH: So, you must have been very surprised with the big reaction because you were very young, right?

HC: I was 23 at the time. Yes, I was surprised. I didn't even think that I would do my own label. I was looking for work.

YH: So, after this you have created many interesting works. For instance you just mentioned about *The Airmail Dress*. This work came about because of this paper? These sequences are quite interesting. Is there something common in this work with your early stage?

HC: That's where it started, in my first collection. That was the first one. I did it in different ways. The jacket, I gave that to Bjork. She used it on her album "Post" cover. Now The Metropolitan Museum or one of the museums in New York has it.

YH: But you never reproduced this one?

HC: No, I just produced it once. And then I took the idea further by doing this series of Air Mail Clothing. I really want to do it again. After that I did T-shirts that you can rip off the package and bits of the package will stay on it. It was really exciting. I really want to do it more. It's fabric but in parts it has paper on it and it's attached to the package. You take it off and a bit of the package stays on the T-shirt. The idea was you can send clothes by post. I wanted them to try it with knitwear, I want to take it further. But it needs money, you know, it needs investment. And then we did it in all different languages on the same envelope, so you can send it anywhere and anyone can read and learn about the concept. I want to revive it.

YH: Do you have any pictures of how it looks like?

HC: It's in the film. You see it in the film *Temporal Meditations* (p.30), you know in the beginning where it's being ripped off.

YH: Because the sequences and how you developed the ideas is like a very beautiful stream. It flows.

HC: I'm obsessed with packaging. I love packaging. I love ripping and tearing. I like the idea. I get excited with clothes being kind of cold and warm. I think I'm cold and warm.

YH: What do you mean by "cold" and "warm"?

HC: Cold and warm meaning, I like the idea that the clothes come from "ideas" which is warm. And then when they're packaged they're cold and impersonal. I love that contrast. Because when they're packaged they're institutional, because I think I'm quite obsessed with institutions. Institutions they prescribe behavior, they prescribe order. And I find it quite exciting somehow. I've always been fascinated by institutions from when I was at St. Martins as well.

YH: Some people say your work is architectural. This is also related to an idea?

HC: I think so, but I'm more interested in the theory of architecture, more than just buildings. I think I'm more interested in the meaning of it. And this is a very good project here that talks about that. This is a very exciting project for me *Place/Non-place* (A/W 2003). This is a menswear project where the buyer of a garment from this collection was invited via the label's text to come to London airport Heathrow at a certain point in time. Here, I wanted the wearers to talk about the life represented by the objects in their pockets. Garments acquire meaning through use and the more memories they contain, the richer the life they have. So the clothes became a token to create an event. Whoever bought the clothes could come. And you know what, one person came. I was shocked. Because by the time the clothes are finished, it takes like almost 9 months, by the time they're in the store. So, he came. One person, and the other day I bumped into him in a supermarket. Actually I didn't meet him at the event, my staff did. But in the supermarket he came up to me and he said, "Are you Hussein? And I said "Yes." And he said "I'm the person... It was shocking.

YH: Very beautiful.

HC: So, basically the idea was that clothes become here a token to meet people. And to create this sort of moment of turning this impersonal space, a waiting room for example, into a kind of mini event, therefore "a place." I find that architectural because it's not about form but it's about the idea of space, what space can mean. Because you're meeting people there and you're making that space into somewhere.

YH: These Aeroplane Dresses are like shields. They look like some kind of protection for the body and they're very structural. What's the idea behind using such hard materials to cover the woman's body?

HC: In this case, it was to reconstruct the body, to keep it upright. Especially there was a surgical corset that I designed. The idea was to keep the body straight. Actually, it was based on Noah's Ark. Because I was trying to connect it to disasters. Like the idea that there was the flood and then there's the ship. In this show I wanted the girls to walk through water, but I couldn't do it. It was supposed to be like post-disaster. I had all these waves and the story was that someone was found a bit injured and we had to keep them upright. So, in a way that's what that was about. And this here, is a similar idea. I'm interested in this surgical reconstructive thing.

YH: Many people talk about the corset.

HC: Some people see it as being quite restricting. However, it's seen in a couple of different ways. I always saw it as reconstructing the body, rather than a restriction. But I don't expect people to walk around like this. This is an idea.

YH: Such as your Aeroplane Dresses in *Echoform* (A/W 1999), or the clothes whose neck is like an upper part of airplane seat, are they based on the same kind of ideas, reconstructing the body?

HC: I think a lot of these things are body-like in the first place. A lot of vehicle designs I think look at the body and in a way imagine the body in hyper speed. So, what I wanted to do was to look at things that I think come from the body, but project it back onto the body.

YH: So, you are talking about the body itself. Even if those kinds of metaphors represent speed and movement, it turns out to be the story of the body itself?

HC: Yes, I was looking at things which come from the body that are in a way amplified from the body but then I put it back onto the body. Architecture, buildings, the way we create systems, the way we build vehicles, everything in a way is like a body. In a way we are recreating the body. What I wanted to do was, take that and then put it back onto the body again. Even a car interior is a negative of the body. Everything we do is an amplification of the body. And I thought why not look at those things and then project it back onto the body. That was really the idea. And the whole project was called *Echoform*.

YH: Your namings are always quite amazing. I think some titles are coined terms. Do you name them by yourself?

HC: Yes, it's a process. Sometimes the name comes by talking to a friend. Often I have an idea and I just bounce it off someone. Really I come up with a name because there is a theme.

YH: Do you have any relationship between the works from *Panoramic* (p.24), which are shown in this exhibition, and the Islamic costumes in *Between* (S/S 1998)? It is a quite symbolical piece in the sense it gets anonymized by concealing one's face.

HC: Actually, *Panoramic* was the collection that followed *Between*. It was a different theme but really this was about trying to deconstruct how we define our territory through belief systems. I think this sort of thing defines territory, especially when you see them on mass. And I was trying to think of how you can dissect it. I liked the idea that it became life and death as well. This was how you were born, and through nurturing you become this and I thought, "This is quite amazing, the fact that it is so simple." And in a way through this Islamic code you are depersonified. This was actually a very important project for me. And this was all before this whole Islamic thing that's happening now. It was very early on. It was about "definition of territory" and "nurture/nature" and "life/death" in a way. Then this one: *Panoramic* was about language and limitations of language. Why language? Because I looked at the idea of how you define things through language and I wanted to create things that you couldn't describe with language. You wouldn't know if it was an ethnic costume or if it was some weird ritualistic clothes. So, what I wanted to do was to create a new uniform that you couldn't define. That's what that was about. That's why they were presented in a mirror, so that they become more echoed and reflected. The body became lost within parameters that you create. So parameters of language, or parameters of culture or belief systems, they're man made but the idea was that we get lost in it ourselves. It was quite complex but I guess that process is for me, in the end people are just looking to see what has come from it. I think processes are there really for the artist/designer. And the result is the important thing for the people. They don't have to know the process.

YH: I'm very curious about your shop. Is it a space where you show your concepts behind collections while you sell clothes which are actually wearable?

HC: Well, people don't have to know the ideas. Honestly if they just like the clothes and think that they are beautiful, that's enough. We just sold some clothes from the collection. But that was the presentation. But in a way the clothes become the components, or in a way the tokens for the show.

YH: But, do you present your performance in the shops using video or something? Do you ever do that?

HC: Yes, I do, if I have a corner. But you know this has been the biggest problem. Really I need my own shop. Not a shop, my space. I don't want to call it a shop because you sell stuff there. But I want it to be more of a space. When we had this temporary store in Tokyo, we had videos upstairs. You could watch the videos. It was a temporary project but still we put a lot of effort into it so we learned as lot from it.

YH: When you opened a new shop in Daikanyama before, I was impressed at the opening where video works were shown and olive trees were offered to visitors. Could you let me know how your works are produced?

HC: Well, I think life is about how you simplify. I think simplifying is the hardest, and I think adding is the easiest. First, I think you have to have an idea but then you have to know how to clean it up. That involves skill. And I think a lot of people who are designers, they add a lot but they don't know how to take away. And you need to know how to take away. It's so difficult.

YH: Do you actually design all your dresses?

HC: I design most things and then I get help because I can't do everything, for example I can't do the technical parts. So, I have a team, of course.

YH: How do you collaborate with your team or outside professional experts? Your works are filled with new imaginations and forms, and so I'm very curious how you share them with others.

HC: I have people that drape for me. I have pattern cutters and I will go to them with an idea and if they start draping I go. Then I change it and they start again, I go and they start again. It's a process and a similar process with the prints, I'll have an idea and then they will do certain things. Then my design team or maybe one person who specializes in that fabrication, she will be able to join the fabric together, or decide what trim we should have. Then I will have a more senior designer, and that person will help me with the fabrics, help me with the range plan, look after the other designers if I'm not there. But for most of the collections; I draw and then I get it developed. But sometimes it's a drawing. Sometimes I go with the fabric and I say I want this done, or I go with a detail and I decide I want to grow the detail. So it really depends on the project. Of course I need people to help me do it. I can't do it on my own, it's impossible.

YH: When you made your moving dresses, you had *111* (p.56), so did you do research?

HC: I had a massive team, of course. I had an electrical engineer, I had a programmer, I had a mechanical engineer, and so on.

YH: But they never worked on creating the dresses, so how did you adopt their work?

HC: It was an experiment. That's why it was expensive and it took so long.

YH: Many people are curious about your great teammates and your cross-disciplinary administration because normally, information or the network is quite limited within the specialized area. Even if you know someone is a robotics expert, you don't know how efficient he or she will be to work with. How do you find just the right person to work with? People are very curious about that.

HC: Yes, it's to do with communication. I think I have good communication skills. And also, I think that if you explain something in the right way, they feel like they are a part of something and I think you get people into it. There's no way I could have done those mechanical dresses on my own, no way.

YH: It's easy to say it's cross-disciplined, but it's not so easy to do, is it? Also, the people doing robotics, they know about mechanics only and they don't know about art and fashion.

HC: Yes, and often they don't have the imagination.

YH: Then please tell me about your work *Before Minus Now* (p.40). This fascinating title is abstract and it seems to have a lot of connotations. What does *Before Minus Now* mean?

HC: It's an abstract kind of title. It was playing with the idea of time. You know how we always talk about the present? Also the project was about forces and gravity and the invisible. I looked at gravity, I looked at magnetic forces and I looked at the electrical force between the object and what you control. I thought that it could be about something that you eat away, something that's invisible that you add to or that you are kind of inspired by that is invisible. I was trying to think of how could I use natural forces as a means to create form? So, I thought "Before Minus." "Now" is this idea that you have form out of nothing. So now, there was nothing and then there was. You took something away or you added something, so I thought it was quite a nice way of playing with the idea of something missing, or something not visible that you can then create something from it so in a way it was a really abstract title.

YH: I think all of your concepts are very sophisticated. Sometimes it's a bit complicated. We can understand the concepts through your collections, films and exhibitions at museums. Regarding the concept, what does 111 years of the title mean?

HC: The whole idea of "movement" started there. And then for *111*, it became much more about changing the era of clothing. It really went a lot further and hopefully my next step is to try to make it completely wearable. That is, that you can buy a garment and then you can actually change it. It's such a big wish of mine. If we could find Japanese sponsors who would sponsor this project, it would be so amazing. The idea is that you can wear a normal jacket and then you can turn it into an evening jacket because you're going out. It's the same jacket but it's designed so you can change it. This would be so exciting. But you need to do it in such a way that you can also wash it.

YH: So, in this collection, what kind of dresses did you present here as wearable clothes? Your collection sometimes consists of monumental dresses for presentation as well as practical dresses together, right?

HC: Yes. The idea is that the monuments really lead to the wearable dresses. And I like this duality of the monumental pieces next to the pieces that have come from them. I find it more modern that in a way, you can extend the life of these monuments by wearing things that are related to them. So, even if I give you a dress, from a collection, you will see some version of it in the more monumental pieces.

YH: Your methodology and your thinking are enlightening many people in the fashion world. The collection show and the concept statement. Do you consider it ideal to have a corner in the shop to present for example by video your monumental works along with presenting your wearable dresses?

HC: Of course. In a way, what we are doing is we're creating a micro-geography with the body and with the clothes, and what we're really doing is showing the monuments as the peak of the process, the ultimate stage of the project. Because that's kind of my pinnacle, everything fits in around it. If I can show something that shows the pinnacle, then I can share the whole project in its entirety rather than just a nice top or a nice shirt. But of course I think it's nice that people can just enjoy the clothes because they're nice clothes. It's the process that has led to their creation, but I think that if I was to have my own shop, or my own corner, ideally, I would show a bit more of the processes, or at least the monuments.

YH: For instance, *After Words* (A/W 2000) collection which is also famous as a performance piece. Could you take it as an example and explain the relationship between monuments and the wearable dresses?

HC: They are related, because it was supposed to be like someone's wardrobe. It was supposed to be a bit "east European." So basically, there was a coat or a dress and they were connected and very similar in shape or the contrast was similar but there were other sections as well. If you see just one section, you might think, oh that's just a dress, how does that relate to the end? But if you see the whole thing, you will see there are always different chapters in a show. The end of this leads to the idea that you're leaving your home behind so you take your final garment covers too, because it was about hiding your possessions during the time of a raid, in wartime. So, if you look only at one part, you might not think there is a connection, you have to see the whole thing. That's why it's a collection. *After Words* was supposed to be like someone's wardrobe, the style of the floral fabrics for instance could have been like someone's wardrode from Eastern Europe. This pattern was also visible in lining of the seat cover dresses which the audience saw being transformed into clothing by the models .The inspiration of this project started off from the war in Kosovo and then I connected it to what happened in Cyprus which was quite similar, when Greek Eoka sympathizers in an attempt to unite Cyprus to Greece were terrorizing Turkish Cypriot homes .The final scenario in the show was about converting the remaining seats into bags and the living room table into a skirt so that one can take all their possessions with them when having to leave their home.

YH: Your entire show is like one performance to convey your ideas to the people. It's a very artistic performance however very limited people can see it because it only happens once.

HC: I think that because I'm a designer, I can't only present this. So, I present clothes within a context. I can't do a collection that's only based on a chair cover because in a way, I think that would limit me too much and also it would mean that I couldn't sell anything from this collection that's just a normal garment. I have to support this by making things that I can sell. So, I have to connect them in different ways. But, that's why when you do a catalogue, it's really important how you edit it. This was the same with the last collection *Mirage* (p.68) that we did. It's supposed to be the wardrobe of someone on an imaginary American road-trip.

YH: Then how about *Earth Bound* (p.64) of 2009?

HC: This was about going into the earth in a way so there are all these cross-sections. It was a reaction to *Inertia* (p.20) the previous season which was all about the earth crashing as a result of speed. *Earthbound* was the opposite, about being in one place and imagining other worlds. I used this fabric because it was quite special. It was like rock. But there was also this sexual charge as well, because you were stationed but also there was this sort of bodily S&M kind of reference as well. I liked that idea of the earthiness but then also the sexual charge. The shoulders are made of moulded leather. So this is again my usual kind of neck thing and the graphicism. This is mixing two different fabrics.

YH: But in the process you make a design and you have ideas about what fabric to use. So the way you described it to me, it's as if you make a sculpture and you know the fabric very well.

HC: Yes. There was a fabric that looks very simple but actually, it was a fabric specially developed for us that went from wool to silk in one go. I like these fabrics that melt from one into another. You can just see a black dress but it was wool and then it went into silk but in one piece, not seamed. The direction I'm going in from the last 3 collections has been to show pieces that you can wear. Actually it's really quite well thought out. But buyers would still consider that to be quite showy. So, recently my energy has gone into show things that you can still wear, but maybe you have to be quite confident to wear them. So, I think ideally what we'll do is we'll have our own environment so that we can... I think I need a space in London, not just a shop but like a space where I can show the clothes and people can come and see them. But people can also buy the clothes. So something like a gallery/shop.

YH: It's where people encounter and experience your concept, which can be called as an alternative model of museum. You are like a re-territorializing catalyst that motivates both art and design. I hope there emerge designers like you from younger generations.

フセイン・チャラヤン インタビュー後記
長谷川祐子

チャラヤンの多才さの秘密について考えたとき、キーワードとして、好奇心、移動、混交、コミュニケーション能力といった言葉が上げられる。

彼が身体を始まりとして、身体にまとう服を通じて大きな文明史観の中で未来、新たな人間性を探究しようとするとき、そこに現れてくる「新しさ」は、ファッション界のいささか狂気じみたスピード、サイクルに足並みを合わせつつも、周りの流行と無関係に彼の独創性から生み出されてくる。

コンセプチュアルと実用的な服の2重性、あるいはその2つの世界の間を横断しながら、チャラヤンの新しさは、彫刻的(モニュメンタル)な服が、着用可能なドレスに導かれていく過程にある。つまりモニュメンタルな服にはコンセプトや知的なエネルギーの素が濃縮されており、そこからはじけた胞子の一つ一つのように、実用的な服があるというイメージだ。中心から泉のように湧き出るそのエッセンスが服を別のものに見せる。また、ショップでなくて「スペース」という表現も、その2重性、横断性をバックアップする考えだ。チャラヤンが「コレクション」という言葉について説明するとき、それは集合知(コレクティブ・インテリジェンス)、とか、集合意識(コレクティブ・コンシャスネス)といった言葉を想起させる。映像や、彫刻的なインスタレーションの中で行われるモニュメンタルなドレスによるパフォーマンス、そして実用的な服を着たモデルたちの登場、それらすべてが、一体となって一つの世界をあらわす、それがチャラヤンの「コレクション」概念だ。

チャラヤンはなぜこのように歴史学や生物学、あるいは科学やテクノロジーという広汎な分野にまたがり領域横断的(クロスディシプリナリー)な創造を展開できるようになったのだろうか？彼はまずそれを周縁、情報や接触を制限された場から来た者の好奇心と説明する。一つの島(キプロス)からイギリスという別のより大きな島への移動、そしてそれぞれに異文化の交流、混交があった。《エアメール・ドレス》、《アフター・ワーズ》の家具のドレス、《場から旅路へ》のロンドンからボスフォラス海峡までを移動する想像上の旅。そして混交は、《不在の存在》(p.36)や《ジオトロピクス》(p.44)でもあらわされている。

セントラル・セント・マーティンス・カレッジ・オブ・アート・アンド・デザインではアーティストや他の専門分野で制作している人が多くいて、ファッションデザインだけでなく、映像制作や彫刻に横断していくことはごく自然な流れだったと言う。

とはいえ、ロボット工学の専門家やエンジニアとともに完成度の高い仕事をするのは容易ではない。チャラヤンはその成功の一因は、自分のコミュニケーション能力の高さにあると言うが、それだけではなく、《111》の動くドレスのように、服がロングからミニへ、つまりソワレから日常着に、歩いている間に自動的に変化してくれたらどんなに素晴らしいかというヴィジョンのきらめきに、関わる人々が魅了され、これを共有することによるのではないか。

地中から掘り出した服に累積した時間の痕跡をつけることから始めた彼は、その重力からの解放を祝福するかのように、無重力の方向に展開した。ここでも重力を幅広いレンジで行き来することでフォームに様々な冒険が生まれている。特に飛行は彼の創造力をかき立て、そのまま回転して飛行体勢に入りそうな、《飛行機ドレス》や、飛行機の翼のインスタレーション、空港を舞台にした映像を作っている。

重力の解釈がそのままフォームになるという考えもそうだが、アイデアは無限の連鎖のようにつながっていく。例えばパッケージについて語っている言葉は、感覚的なものが服作りという物理的な過程を経て、政治や社会、機構や規律、思想に接続され、止揚されていくという、彼の哲学の表明である。洋服の原点は「温かい」が、一度パッケージされると「冷たく」なる。そのコントラスト、私的でやわらかなものが突然機構的になる変化への関心。彼は「パッケージ」をし、それを破いたりはがしたりして楽しむ。その仕事はなしくずしに行なわれることはなく、構築的で、生産的だ。

チャラヤンは、直感的に対象のエッセンスを把握する。建築のセオリーとは何かについて彼は解読しながら、《場所でない場所》プロジェクトで、服につけたラベルのメッセージに従って行動した人々によって作られた出会いのスペースと時間に「建築的な」意味を見出し、洋服がある出来事を創出する「しるし」となると言う。

そこでは「空間の形成」を「意味の形成」と同義にみなしている、彼の明快さがある。チャラヤンの服はミニマルというより、シンプルな原理に基づいて作られている。彼はシンプルにそぎ落とすことの大切さと難しさを言うが、服が起点となり、意味が生産されるという大きなヴィジョンの枠の中で、このことは彼にとって困難なことではないだろう。彼は服を「生きられた哲学」にしたクリエイターの一人である。

長谷川祐子 | Yuko Hasegawa

東京都現代美術館チーフキュレーター。京都大学法学部卒業後、東京芸術大学大学院美術研究科修士課程修了。水戸芸術館、ニューヨークのホイットニー美術館研修、世田谷美術館を経て、金沢21世紀美術館学芸課長(1999–2005)、芸術監督(2005–2006)を務める。2006年4月より現職。多摩美術大学芸術学科特任教授及び芸術人類学研究所所員。第7回イスタンブール・ビエンナーレ総合コミッショナー(2001年)、第4回上海ビエンナーレ コ・キュレーター(2002年)、第50回ヴェネチア・ビエンナーレ日本館コミッショナー(2003年)、第29回サンパウロ・ビエンナーレ コ・キュレーター(2010年)などを務めたほか、「マシュー・バーニー:拘束のドローイング」(2005–06年、金沢21世紀美術館)、「SPACE FOR YOUR FUTURE:アートとデザインの遺伝子を組み替える」(2007–2008年)、「ネオ・トロピカリア:ブラジルの創造力」(2008–09年、ともに東京都現代美術館)などを企画する。

Hussein Chalayan Interview Afterword
Yuko Hasegawa

Chalayan's many talents, how can we describe them? Some words that come to mind are curiosity, hybridity and skill in communication.

He uses the body and the clothing on it to explore humankind's future. His viewpoints, based on a deep understanding of the great history of civilization, present us a fresh outlook on human nature. The resulting "newness" of his works keeps pace with the frenetic speed and cycles of the fashion world while also producing his own unique style.

While his garments are both conceptual and practical, or a cross between those two worlds, Chalayan's newness lies in a process by which monumental garments become wearable dresses. In other words, his monumental garments are rich in concepts and intellectual energy, and practical garments pop up from these designs like one spore after another. The essence that flows from their core like a fountain turns his garments into something else entirely. His usage of the word "space" instead of "shop" backs up this duality and sense of crossing between the two. When Chalayan explains the word "collection", he evokes the words "collective intelligence" and "collective consciousness". The monumental dresses in his films and monumental installations, and the appearance of the models in his practical dresses all become one and represent one world: that is the concept of Chalayan's collections.

How did Chalayan become able to produce these cross-disciplinary creations that straddle a wide range of areas such as history and biology or science and technology? He begins by explaining the curiosity of somebody from the place where information and contact to the world were limited. He moved from one island (Cyprus) to Britain, another, bigger island, and experienced an exchange and blending of different cultures. This can be seen in *Airmail Dress* and *After Words*, his furniture dresses, and *Place to Passage*, an imagined journey from London to the Bosphorus. The blending can also be seen in *The Absent Presence* (p.36) and *Geotropics* (p.44). Chalayan says that Central Saint Martins College of Art and Design is full of artists and people producing works in other specialist areas, and the crossing over from fashion design to film production and installations was a natural progression.

That being said, it is not easy to do a job with the same level of perfectionism as robotics and engineering. Chalayan says that one reason for his success is his great skill in communication, but there must be more to it than that. He possesses both the ability to charm those he associates with but he also has wonderful flashes of inspiration that lead him to garments such as *111*. A moving dress from *111* is that automatically changes from a long dress to a mini-dress – and thereby from formal to everyday – as the wearer walks.

He began with garments dug up from the earth bearing the vestiges of time, and then moved on to weightlessness, as if celebrating liberation from gravity. Flight in particular aroused his creativity, leading him to produce his *Aeroplane Dress* which looked like it was taking flight as the model turned. He also produced installations of aeroplane wings and films set at airports.

Those who think that his interpretation of gravity simply lent itself to forms are right, but it was the result of an endless chain of ideas. For example, the words he uses to describe packaging are a manifestation of his philosophy that throughout the physical process of clothing making, sensory things connect with politics and society, structure and discipline and thought and then sublate. Clothing has warm origins, but once packaged it becomes "cold". He is interested in the contrast, the way something soft in private suddenly becomes institutional. He packages things and then enjoys ripping or peeling the packaging off. He does not do this gradually but in a constructive and productive way.

Chalayan instinctively ascertains the essences he is looking for. He says that in his *Place/Non-Place* project he deciphered the meaning of architectural theory while finding an "architectural" meaning in a space and time in which people create encounters with each other by following messages on clothing labels, and that this is a "token" that clothing can create events.

This possesses Chalayan's lucidity in regarding "formation of space" to be synonymous with "formation of meaning". Rather than being minimalistic, Chalayan's garments are made based on simple principles. He talks about the importance and difficulty of trimming down to something simple, but this is surely not hard for him within the bounds of his vision in which clothing is the starting point for creating meaning. He is one creator who has made clothing into a living philosophy.

Yuko Hasegawa

Yuko Hasegawa is a Chief Curator of the Museum of Contemporary Art Tokyo (MOT). She is also a professor of the Department of Art Science, Tama Art University in Tokyo. Her recent projects are "When Lives Become Form: Contemporary Brazilian Art: 1960s to the Present" (2008) and "SPACE FOR YOUR FUTURE: Recombining DNA of Art and Design" (2007) at the Museum of Contemporary Art Tokyo. At the 21st Century Museum of Contemporary Art, Kanazawa where she was appointed as a Founding Artistic Director, she curated the inaugural exhibition "Polyphony" (2004) and "Matthew Barney—Drawing Restraint" (2005). She was also appointed as Artistic Director of the 7th International Istanbul Biennial (2001), Co-Curator of the 4th Shanghai Biennale (2002), and commissioner of Japanese Pavilion of 50th Venice Biennale (2003), Co-curator of the29 th Sao Paulo Biennale (2010).

フセイン・チャラヤン略歴

1970	キプロス島ニコシア生まれ
1982	ロンドンの寄宿学校に入学
1993	ロンドンのセントラル・セント・マーティンズ・カレッジ・オブ・アート・アンド・デザイン、ファッション専攻科卒業。卒業制作で発表したコレクションが後にロンドンの老舗ブティック、ブラウンズのショーウィンドウを飾る
1994	自身のブランドを立ち上げる
1995	ロンドン・ファッション・ウィークで初めてのコレクションを発表する
	第1回アブソルート・ウォッカ、アブソルート・クリエイション・デザイン・アワード受賞
1998	ニューヨークのカシミア会社セイ(TSE)でデザイン担当 (2001年まで)
	マイケル・クラーク作品《Current/See》で衣装デザイン担当
1999	ニューヨークでエリック・フラード制作、ヘンデルの《メサイア》の衣装デザイン担当
	英国ファッション・アワードのデザイナー・オブ・ザ・イヤー受賞
2000	ロンドンの一般向け小売業トップ・ショップとマークス&スペンサーでコレクションをプロデュース
	英国ファッション・アワードのデザイナー・オブ・ザ・イヤーを2年連続受賞
2001	ロンドンの宝飾店アスプレイのクリエイティヴ・ディレクター就任
2002	パリ・コレクションへの参加を開始
	初のメンズウエア・コレクションを立ち上げる
	ベルギーで『Cマガジン』を立ち上げ、編集に携わる
2004	東京・代官山に旗艦店オープン
2006	ファッション業界への貢献により大英帝国勲章MBEを受勲
2007	ロンドンのデザイン・ミュージアムでブリット・インシュランス・デザイン・オブ・ザ・イヤーをファッション部門で受賞
	ニューヨークのファッション・グループ・インターナショナルでナイト・オブ・スターズ・アワードを受賞
2008	ロンドンにてプーマと提携、クリエイティヴ・ディレクター就任

コレクション歴

1994	秋冬コレクション	「デカルト派」
1995	春夏コレクション	「一時的な妨害」
	秋冬コレクション	「偽りの赤道に沿って」
1996	春夏コレクション	「無/インタースコープ」
	秋冬コレクション	「静物」
1997	春夏コレクション	「ランズ・ウィズアウト」
	秋冬コレクション	「嵐の香り」
1998	春夏コレクション	「ビトウィーン」
	秋冬コレクション	「パノラマ」
1999	春夏コレクション	「ジオトロピクス」
	秋冬コレクション	「エコーフォーム」
2000	春夏コレクション	「ビフォア・マイナス・ナウ」
	秋冬コレクション	「アフター・ワーズ」
2001	春夏コレクション	「腹話術」
	秋冬コレクション	「マップリーディング」
2002	春夏コレクション	「メディア」
	秋冬コレクション	「アンビモルファス」
2003	春夏コレクション	「明白なる運命」
	秋冬コレクション	「類縁の旅」
2004	春夏コレクション	「束の間の瞑想」
	秋冬コレクション	「孤独の人類学」
2005	春夏コレクション	「ブラインドスケープ」
	秋冬コレクション	「ゲノメトリクス」
2006	春夏コレクション	「ヘリオトロピクス」
	秋冬コレクション	「休息」
2007	春夏コレクション	「111」
	秋冬コレクション	「エアボーン」
2008	春夏コレクション	「リーディングス」
	秋冬コレクション	「粒子と鋼」
2009	春夏コレクション	「慣性」
	秋冬コレクション	「地からは離れられない」
2010	春夏コレクション	「無為な日々を過ごす甘美さ」
	秋冬コレクション	「ミラージュ」

展覧会歴

主な個展

- 1996 ウィンドウ・ギャラリー／プラハ
- 1998 コレット／パリ
- 2003 「アンビモルファス」(アントワープ・ファッション美術館)
  「束の間の瞑想」(ペルゴラ劇場／フィレンツェ、パレ・ド・トーキョー／パリ)
- 2004 「場から旅路へ」(現代美術センター／ジュネーヴ)
- 2005 「フセイン・チャラヤン」(フローニンゲン美術館／オランダ)
  第51回ヴェネツィア・ビエンナーレ(トルコ館／ヴェネツィア)
- 2009 「フセイン・チャラヤン――ファッションにはじまり、そしてファッションへ戻る旅」(デザイン・ミュージアム／ロンドン)

主なグループ展

- 1996 「ジャム:スタイル+音楽+メディア」(バービカン・アートギャラリー／ロンドン)
- 1997 「カッティング・エッジ」(ヴィクトリア・アンド・アルバート美術館／ロンドン)
- 1998 「今世紀を語る:100年間の美術とファッション」(ヘイワードギャラリー／ロンドン)
- 1999 「身体の夢――ファッションOR見えないコルセット」(京都国立近代美術館、東京都現代美術館)
- 2000 「美」(アヴィニョン)
- 2001 第7回イスタンブール・ビエンナーレ
  「ジャム―東京―ロンドン」(バービカン・アートギャラリー／ロンドン)
  「センチュリー・シティ」(テート・モダン／ロンドン)
  「大いなる期待」(グランド・セントラル・ステーション／ニューヨーク)
  「ラディカル・ファッション」(ヴィクトリア・アンド・アルバート美術館／ロンドン)
- 2003 「女神:ザ・クラシカル・モード」(ニューヨーク近代美術館)
- 2004 「21世紀の出会い――共鳴、ここ・から」(金沢21世紀美術館)
  「スキン・タイト――肉体の感覚」(シカゴ現代美術館)
- 2006 「スキン+ボーンズ――1980年代以降の建築とファッション」(ロサンゼルス現代美術館、国立新美術館／東京、2007年)
- 2007 「SPACE FOR YOUR FUTURE――アートとデザインの遺伝子を組み替える」(東京都現代美術館)

Biography

1970	Born in Nicosia, Cyprus.	
1982	Attends boarding school in London.	
1993	Graduates with a BA Hons in Fashion from Central St. Martins College of Art and Design, London. Graduate collection later features in the window of London retailer, Browns.	
1994	Launches own label.	
1995	Shows debut collection at London Fashion Week. Winner of the first Absolut Vodka, Absolut Creation Design Award.	
1998	Designs for New York cashmere company, Tse (1998–2001). Designs costumes for Michael Clark's production of Current/See.	
1999	Designs costumes for Eric Fraad's production of Handel's Messiah in New York. Named British Designer of the Year.	
2000	Produces collections for the London high street retailers, Top Shop and M&S. Named British Designer of the Year for the second successive year.	
2001	Appointed Creative Director of Asprey, London.	
2002	Begins to show collections in Paris. Launches first menswear collection. Launches and edits C magazine, Belgium.	
2004	Opens flagship store in Daikanyama, Tokyo.	
2006	Awarded MBE for services to the fashion industry.	
2007	Wins the Fashion category: Brit Insurance Designs of the Year at the Design Museum, London. Wins Night of Stars award, Fashion Group International, New York.	
2008	Appointed Creative Director and partners with Puma, London.	

1994	Autumn/Winter	Cartesia
1995	Spring/Summer	Temporary Interference
	Autumn/Winter	Along False Equator
1996	Spring/Summer	Nothing/Interscape
	Autumn/Winter	Still Life
1997	Spring/Summer	Lands Without
	Autumn/Winter	Scent of Tempests
1998	Spring/Summer	Between
	Autumn/Winter	Panoramic
1999	Spring/Summer	Geotropics
	Autumn/Winter	Echoform
2000	Spring/Summer	Before Minus Now
	Autumn/Winter	After Words
2001	Spring/Summer	Ventriloquy
	Autumn/Winter	Mapreading
2002	Spring/Summer	Medea
	Autumn/Winter	Ambimorphous
2003	Spring/Summer	Manifest Destiny
	Autumn/Winter	Kinship Journeys
2004	Spring/Summer	Temporal Meditations
	Autumn/Winter	Anthropology of Solitude
2005	Spring/Summer	Blindscape
	Autumn/Winter	Genometrics
2006	Spring/Summer	Heliotropics
	Autumn/Winter	Repose
2007	Spring/Summer	One Hundred and Eleven
	Autumn/Winter	Airborne
2008	Spring/Summer	Readings
	Autumn/Winter	Grains and Steel
2009	Spring/Summer	Inertia
	Autumn/Winter	Earthbound
2010	Spring/Summer	Dolce Far Niente
	Autumn/Winter	Mirage

Collections

Exhibitions

Selected solo exhibitions

- 1996 The Window Gallery, Prague
- 1998 Colette, Paris
- 2003 *Ambimorphous*, Antwerp Fashion Museum
  Temporal Meditations, Teatro della Pergola, Florence; Palais de Tokyo
- 2004 *Place to Passage*, Centre d'Art Contemporain, Geneve
- 2005 Groninger Museum, Groningen
  51st Venice Binnale, Turkish Pavilion, Venice
- 2009 *Hussein Chalayan - from fashion and back*, Design Museum, London

Selected group exhibitions

- 1996 *Jam – Style + Music + Media*, Barbican Art Gallery, London
- 1997 *The Cutting Edge*, Victoria and Albert Museum, London
- 1998 *Addressing the Century: 100 Years of Art & Fashion*, Hayward Gellery, London
- 1999 *Visions of the Body: Fashion or Invisible Corset*, The Museum of Modern Art, Kyoto; Museum of Contemporary Art, Tokyo
- 2000 *La Beaute*, Avignon
- 2001 *7th Istanbul Biennalé*
  Jam: Tokyo - London, Barbican Art Gallery, London
  Century City, Tate Modern, London
  Great Expectations, Grand Central Terminal, New York
  Radical Fashion, Victoria and Albert Museum, London
- 2003 *Goddess: The Classical Mode*, Museum of Modern Art, New York
- 2004 *The Encounters in the 21st Century: Polyphony – Emerging Resounance*, 21st Century Museum of Contemporary Art, Kanazawa
  Skin Tight: The Sensibility of the Flesh, Museum of Contemporary Art, Chicago
- 2006 *Skin + Bones: Parallel Practices in Fashion and Architecture*, The Museum of Contemporary Art, Los Angeles; The National Art Center, Tokyo (2007)
- 2007 *SPACE FOR YOUR FUTURE - Recombining the DNA of Art and Design*, Museum of Contemporary Art Tokyo

フセイン・チャラヤン
ファッションにはじまり、そしてファッションへ戻る旅

会期：2010年4月3日 — 6月20日
会場：東京都現代美術館
主催：公益財団法人東京都歴史文化財団 東京都現代美術館
助成：ブリティッシュ・カウンシル
　　　財団法人朝日新聞文化財団
協力：KLMオランダ航空
後援：トルコ共和国大使館
企画：デザイン・ミュージアム［イギリス、ロンドン］

展覧会企画：
長谷川祐子［東京都現代美術館］
吉﨑和彦［東京都現代美術館］
ドナ・ラブデー［デザイン・ミュージアム］

企画コンサルタント：マーク・ウィルソン［フローニンゲン美術館］
展覧会構成：ブロック・アーキテクチャー
広報宣伝デザイン：近藤一弥［Kazuya Kondo Inc.］

———
この展覧会の実現に当たり、貴重な作品をご出品いただいた下記の皆様に深く感謝の意を表します。（順不同・敬称略表記）

フローニンゲン美術館、オランダ
グラン＝デューク・ジャン近代美術館［MUDAM］、ルクセンブルグ
ハン・ネフキンス
スワロフスキー、ロンドン

本展開催にあたり、多大なご協力を賜りました下記関係者・関係機関の皆様に深甚なる感謝の意を表します。（順不同・敬称略表記）

ミリー・パトザレック［フセイン・チャラヤン・スタジオ］
クラウディア・ボーテ［フセイン・チャラヤン・スタジオ］
市川真樹［フセイン・チャラヤン・スタジオ］
リア・ホーソン［デザイン・ミュージアム］
ゾエ・スミス［ブロック・アーキテクチャー］
アンナ・チャップマン［スワロフスキー］
ABAKE
パトリック・セイラー［スワロフスキー］
クリエイティブ・プーマ・ドット・コム
マリー・ノエレ・ファーシー［グラン＝デューク・ジャン近代美術館］
ディビット・ブログマン［グラン＝デューク・ジャン近代美術館］
ムラート・ピレフネリ［ガレリスト、トルコ］
マーカス・トムリンソン
ニュートラル

———

Hussein Chalayan
from fashion and back

Date: April 3 – June 20, 2010
Venue: Museum of Contemporary Art Tokyo [MOT]
Organized by: Tokyo Metropolitan Foundation for History and Culture, Museum of Contemporary Art Tokyo
Supported by: the British Council,
The Asahi Shimbun Foundation
In Cooperation With: KLM Royal Dutch Airlines
Under the patronage of: The Embassy of
the Republic of Turkey
Planning: Design Museum [London]
A touring exhibition from the Design Museum, London.

Exhibition Curators:
Yuko Hasegawa [Museum of Contemporary Art Tokyo]
Kazuhiko Yoshizaki [Museum of Contemporary Art Tokyo]
Donna Loveday [Design Museum]

Curatorial Consultant: Mark Wilson [Groninger Museum]
Exhibition Design: Block Architecture
Promotional Art Direction by: Kazuya Kondo [Kazuya Kondo Inc.]

———

Special thanks to Milly Patrzalek, Claudia Bothe, Maki Ichikawa, Hussein Chalayan Studio; Ria Hawthorn, Design Museum; Zoe Smith, Block Architecture; ABAKE

Museum of Contemporary Art, Tokyo would like to thank all lenders to this exhibition:
Groninger Museum, The Netherlands
MUDAM, Luxembourg
Han Nefkens
Swarovski, London

And to:
Anna Chapman and Patrick Seiler, Swarovski
creative.puma.com
Marie-Noëlle Farcy and David Brognan, MUDAM
Murat Pilevneli, Galerist
Marcus Tomlinson
Katsuya Shirakawa

With thanks to Neutral for all their work on Place to Passage and to Alexandra Scherillo

Image credit

A
Adrian Wilson
Courtesy of Hussein Chalayan
B
Chris Moore
C
Courtesy of Hussein Chalayan
D
Chris Moore
E
Marcus Tomlinson p.26
Film still courtesy of Hussein Chalayan p.27
F
Chris Moore
G
Film still courtesy of Hussein Chalayan p.30
Chris Moore p.31
H
Chris Moore
I
Thierry Bal p.36
Courtesy of Hussein Chalayan
J
Nick Knight
K
Chris Moore
L
Chris Moore
M
Marcus Tomlinson p.44
Chris Moore p.45
N
Courtesy of Hussein Chalayan
O
Film still courtesy of Hussein Chalayan / Neutral
P
Chris Moore
Q
Chris Moore
R
Chris Moore
S
Film still courtesy of Hussein Chalayan p.58
Marcus Tomlinson p.59
T
Chris Moore
U
Chris Moore
V
Chris Moore
W
Chris Moore

Cover (*Ariborn*, A/W 2007)
Photograph by Luke Hayes
Riverse of The Cover
Photograph by Chris Moore
Courtesy of Hussein Chalayan

Photographs by
Kenta Yoshizawa
pp.9-17, pp.34-35, pp.54-55, pp.70-71, p.75, p.83
Keizo Kioku
p.20, P.32, pp.62-63

フセイン・チャラヤン
ファッションにはじまり、そしてファッションへ戻る旅

2010年5月15日初版第1刷発行

編集：
長谷川祐子［東京都現代美術館］
吉﨑和彦［東京都現代美術館］
押金純士［株式会社美術出版社］
友永文博［パッド株式会社］
髙城昭夫［パッド株式会社］
名古摩耶

編集補：西翼
翻訳：アールアイシー出版株式会社
AD・デザイン：近藤一弥［Kazuya Kondo Inc.］
DTP：一瀬貴之［Kazuya Kondo Inc.］
プリンティング・ディレクター：花岡秀明［株式会社オノウエ印刷］

印刷・製本：株式会社オノウエ印刷

発行者：大下健太郎
発行所：株式会社美術出版社
〒101-8417 東京都千代田区神田神保町2-38 稲岡九段ビル8階
Tel.03-3234-2173 Fax.03-3234-1365

価格はカバーに表示してあります。
乱丁、落丁本はお手数ですが、小社宛にお送りください。
送料小社負担にて取り替えいたします。

ISBN978-4-568-10386-1 C3070

禁無断複写
©Hussein Chalayan, Bijutsu Shuppan-Sha 2010

Hussein Chalayan
from fashion and back

First Edition April 28, 2010

Editors:
Yuko Hasegawa [Museum of Contemporary Art Tokyo]
Kazuhiko Yoshizaki [Museum of Contemporary Art Tokyo]
Junji Oshigane [Bijutsu Shuppan-Sha Co., Ltd.]
Fumihiro Tomonaga [pad Inc.]
Akio Takashiro [pad Inc.]
Maya Nago

Editorial Assistant: Tsubasa Nishi
Translation: R.I.C. Publications
Art Direction & Design: Kazuya Kondo [Kazuya Kondo Inc.]
DTP Operation: Takayuki Ichinose [Kazuya Kondo Inc.]
Printing Director: Hideaki Hanaoka [Onoue Printings Inc.]

Printed by: Onoue Printings Inc.

Publisher: Kentaro Oshita
Bijutsu Shuppan-Sha Co., Ltd.
Inaokakudan Bldg. 2-38 Kanda Jinbo-cho Chiyoda-ku Tokyo 101-8417

All rights reserved. No part of this publication may be reproduced or transmitted in any form or by any means. Without prior permission in writing from Hussein Chalayan and Bujitsu Shuppan-Sha.